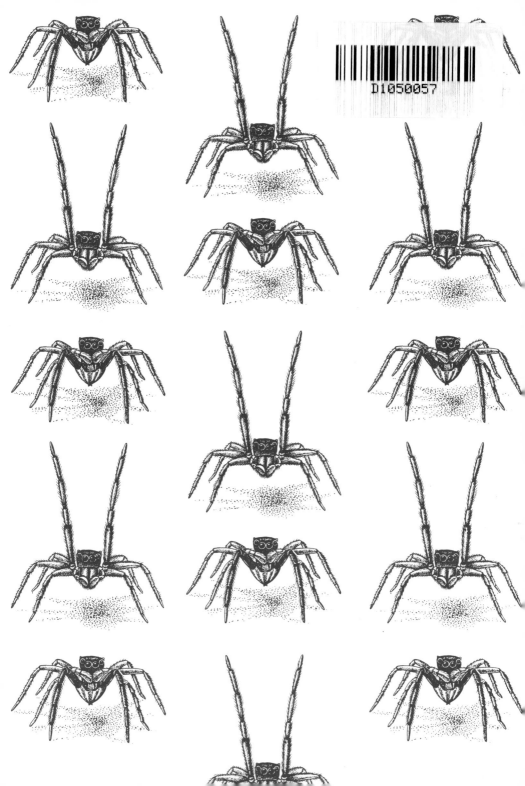

SPIDERS

Eurypelma mesomelas, *a typical mygalomorph or bird-eating spider.*

SPIDERS

Michael Chinery

WITH ILLUSTRATIONS BY SOPHIE ALLINGTON

Whittet Books

(ENDPAPER ILLUSTRATION) jumping spider

First published 1993
Text © 1993 by Michael Chinery
Illustrations © 1993 by Sophie Allington

Whittet Books Ltd, 18 Anley Road, London W14 0BY

The rights of Michael Chinery and Sophie Allington to be identified as the authors of
this work have been asserted in accordance with the Copyright, Designs and Patents
Act 1988

Design by Richard Kelly

British Library Cataloguing in Publication Data
A catalogue record for this book is available from the British Library

ISBN 1 873580 09 6

Typeset by Litho Link Ltd, Welshpool, Powys, Wales
Printed and bound by Biddles of Guildford

CONTENTS

Introduction

If Little Miss Muffet had been a little bit braver and, instead of running away, had stayed sitting on her tuffet to watch the spider that dropped in for lunch, she might have seen it in a very different light. Instead of a scary, eight-legged monster, she could have seen a true artisan at work with the finest silk. An orb-web spider, which was Miss Muffet's most likely companion, can dispense and manipulate a hundred yards or more of silk and produce its intricate web – often more than a yard across and containing perhaps a thousand connections – in under an hour. And it does all this without a single lesson, relying on that mysterious phenomenon that we call instinct. The fact that a flimsy web can support a spider and snare prey weighing several thousand times as much as the web itself testifies to the excellence of the design and of the materials used in its construction.

The construction of an orb-web is surely one of the most amazing of all animal feats, and it is one that I never tire of watching, but spider creativity and inventiveness does not stop at the design and building of webs. Many species are superb hunters, using a wide range of techniques involving stealth, camouflage and agility to capture an equally wide range of prey. Even piracy and common theft figure in the lifestyles of some spiders. Almost all spiders slay their victims by injecting them with poison. Maturity brings the inevitable passion for sex, and in this field the spiders' inventiveness does not lag too far behind that seen in our so-called adult movies! And when all that is over many spiders make a pretty good fist of parental care.

Although not all spiders actually make webs to trap their prey, silk of one kind or another is at the heart of virtually all spider activity and you cannot watch a spider for very long without seeing its silk put to good use. Most spiders use silk to immobilize and wrap their victims, and few spiders ever go anywhere without trailing a few strands of silk behind them to serve as life-lines. Silk is also used to line the burrows of ground-living species, and all spiders protect their eggs by wrapping them in silken parcels.

A fear of spiders
Little Miss Muffet, whom W.S. Bristowe identified as Patience, the daughter of the distinguished 16th-century naturalist Thomas Muffet, was not the first person to flee from a spider and she certainly was not the last: thousands of people suffer from arachnophobia – the posh name for the fear of spiders – and will do anything they can to avoid coming into contact with the animals. Whether an afternoon of spider-watching would have cured Miss Muffet's fear of spiders is impossible to say, but people with severe arachnophobia have often been helped by a process of habituation, during which they are introduced *very gradually* to the animals, starting with pictures of them perhaps and working up to the real thing – in closed containers and at a distance at first, but moved progressively nearer until the patient can touch them. The fear is removed, or at least greatly diminished, and by learning something of the fascinating lives and habits of the spiders a patient often develops a sneaking admiration for the animals. So read on.

If your aversion to spiders is nothing stronger than a dislike of the large ones that run around in the house, try calling them by a different name. I recently heard my son tell his wife that there was a Sydney in the kitchen. I obviously looked puzzled, and was informed that spiders, which had previously caused some consternation, are now known as Sydneys and, although they are still ejected in due course, there is no frantic rush to remove them.

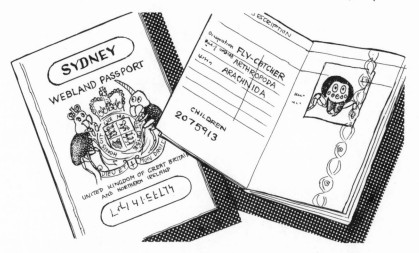

The reason for such widespread fear and dislike of spiders is difficult to uncover. Some spiders certainly have exceedingly toxic venoms and are capable of producing great pain or even death with a single bite, but only about 30 of the 40,000 or so known kinds of spiders are really dangerous to human life and none of these occurs in the British Isles. The Ancient Greeks and Romans were aware of the Mediterranean black widow, whose bite is extremely painful, although rarely fatal, but most of the really dangerous spiders occur in Australia and the Americas and cannot be responsible for the long-standing, global aversion to these eight-legged creatures.

Despite this universal dislike of spiders, there is in most human societies a recognition that it is unlucky to kill the animals, and people all over the world tend to obey the old rhyme

If you wish to live and thrive
Let a spider run alive.

This idea probably stems from the usefulness of spiders in killing and eating troublesome flies and other insects, and Bristowe, in his absorbing book, *The World of Spiders*, quotes several old poems which refer to this facet of spider life. The following rhyme from the north of England sums it up pretty well:

Kill a spider, bad luck yours will be
Until of flies you've swatted fifty-three.

Spiders everywhere

Whether you like them or hate them, the one thing that is certain is that you can never really get away from spiders. They are everywhere. Fields, woods, deserts, caves and gardens are full of them, and many invade our houses in search of food and shelter. James Bond even finds them in his bed – but only when they've been put there. Most spiders are far more likely to move away from people, although some people have been bitten in their beds (see p. 43). Golden orb-web spiders festoon the tropical forests with webs as tough as fishing nets, while other species scramble about on the seashore. Several spiders hunt on the surface of ponds and streams and the unique water spider spends almost all of its life under the surface. Quite a few spiders live in the nests of ant and termites, and several have successfully transferred from beaches and marshland to sewage filter beds – where there are always plenty of flies for them to eat. But the prize for resourcefulness must go to some little crab spiders of the genus *Misumenops*. These spiders live only in the traps of various pitcher plants, where they steal some of the flies destined for the soup that accumulates in each pitcher.

Wolf spiders of various kinds prowl over the northern tundra as soon as the snow melts for the short summer – and sometimes even before it melts – and there are even spiders living over 20,000 feet up on Mount Everest, feeding on springtails around the edges of the snow. These insects, which feed on the drizzle of pollen and other debris blown up there by the wind, are so numerous in some places that they turn the snow black. Even remote islands have their spiders – carried there perhaps by air currents (see page 98) or as stowaways on floating logs. Ships also transport plenty of spiders, including the various 'banana spiders', such as *Heteropoda venatoria*, that travel the world in consignments of bananas and other fruit and sometimes manage to establish themselves, if only temporarily, far from their native haunts.

Sitting in a restaurant on a Reykjavik quayside one evening, I did my Robert the Bruce impression and watched a female *Zygiella x-notata* struggling to fix her web to the window frame. My cod arrived with its prawn stuffing and I thought little more about the spider until I discovered that the species had not previously been recorded in Iceland: my specimen had almost certainly arrived on a ship. Only Antarctica seems to be entirely free from spiders.

Huge numbers

No-one who strolls along a country lane or across rough grassland on an autumn morning can fail to appreciate the prodigious amount of silk draping the vegetation. I think I first became aware of the size of the spider

population when I was at primary school. The footpath leading to the school was bounded by thick hedges which, on autumn mornings, were draped with sparkling, dew-laden webs. I don't think I ever counted them, but there were a lot and my friends and I amused ourselves on the way to school by collecting them on slender loops made from privet twigs. The sticky webs clung to the twigs and, with the dew trapped among the fine strands of silk, they eventually made a primitive sort of mirror – a bit like a soap film on a loop of wire. We used to have competitions to see who had the best one when we arrived at school. A really good one could be used to bounce a ping-pong ball, so we must have learned something about the elasticity of spider silk. There must have been a lot of hungry spiders along that footpath, because we took the webs quite regularly.

More recently, on about an acre of rough grassland in France, I discovered a dense population of the beautiful yellow-and-black orb-web spider *Argiope bruennichi*. But this time I preferred just to watch. As the sun swept across the field in the morning the grasshoppers sprang into life – and many of them sprang straight into the spiders' webs, where they were quickly trussed. Some spiders had three or four such meals in their webs, and I was not surprised to see that some of the spiders were nearly twice as long as the 15mm (0.6 inch) quoted in the books. I did not count all the webs, but there must have been several thousand of them, shimmering like new bicycle wheels in the sunshine. But Bristowe *did* count spiders and their webs, and estimated that an acre of rough grassland may contain over 2,250,000 spiders in the autumn. That's over 5½ million spiders to the hectare. Most of them are, of course, midgets of the money-spider variety with very small appetites, but these huge populations obviously play a major role in the economy of nature. Several keen mathematicians have tried to work out what weight of insects and other small creatures is destroyed by spiders each year. It's an impossible task, of course, but if we assume that the average daily catch is just 1mg of insects and springtails for each spider – a not unreasonable assumption in view of the abundance of tiny money spiders in the population – we arrive at a figure of 5.5kg of flesh devoured each day by the spiders on our hectare of autumn grassland. Take it from there if you like, but don't forget that spider populations fluctuate widely through the year.

Spidery form

THE SPIDER'S PEDIGREE

If spiders could understand human speech they would undoubtedly suffer from identity crises, because many people wrongly allude to them as insects. Although insects and spiders both belong to the huge group of animals known as the arthropods – all with jointed limbs – they are not closely related and you don't need an A-level in biology to distinguish them. An insect's body is usually clearly divided into three parts and it bears six legs and a pair of feelers or antennae. Wings are usually present, although there are plenty of wingless insects – including many ants. Spiders, on the other hand, have four pairs of legs and only two body sections. They never have wings or antennae, although a pair of slender palps in front of the legs act like antennae and could be mistaken for them.

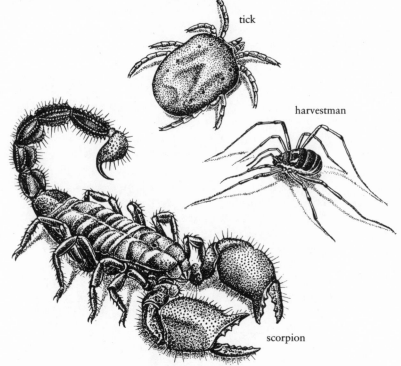

tick

harvestman

scorpion

Some spidery relatives

Spiders belong to the class of arthropods known as the Arachnida, and they share it with the scorpions, mites, harvestmen (see page 118), and a motley assemblage of other leggy creatures. All are essentially 8-legged, but this is one of the few features that they have in common. There are about 12 orders of living arachnids – depending on whose scheme of classification you consult – and the spiders all belong to the order Araneae. They differ from all other arachnids in having venomous fangs, technically known as chelicerae, just in front of the mouth. In nearly all the other arachnid orders the chelicerae are like tiny forceps and are used to crush and tear the prey, although they have no venom. Spiders are also the only arachnids with silk-producing glands in their hind quarters. The extraordinary sea spiders, which have been described as 'all legs and no body', used to be arachnids, but are now placed in a separate class of arthropods known as the Pycnogonida and they are not spiders at all – another identity crisis.

Spiders are pretty ancient creatures and have been wandering around the world for a very long time. The first ones, as far as we can tell from the few fossil spiders that have been unearthed, existed during the Devonian Period, about 400 million years ago. They must have evolved from some aquatic creature – perhaps one that lived in shallow water and was forced on to the land by the gradual shrinking of the Devonian seas and lakes, but we know nothing of these hypothetical spider ancestors. Spiders were undoubtedly abundant in the coal forests of the Carboniferous Period, about 300 million years ago, but, being soft-bodied creatures, they left few fossils. We have to make a giant leap through time to the Cretaceous Period, about 140 million years ago, to find the next fossils of any significance – minute fossils from a Spanish quarry with claws that suggest they were orb-web spinners. And then nothing until the Oligocene Epoch, a mere 35 million years ago, whose fossils – most of them preserved in amber – are very like the spiders that we see around us today. So there are some pretty big gaps in our knowledge of the stages by which modern spiders evolved from the early ones.

More than 40,000 spider species are known today, ranging from giant 'bird-eaters', whose legs would cover a dinner plate, to midgets whose bodies would not even cover a pin-head. Thousands more species undoubtedly await discovery. Even in Great Britain, where spiders have been fairly well studied, about 50 new species have been discovered since 1950. Thousands of unknown species must exist in the tropical forests, but at the current rate of forest destruction – 142,200 sq. km of tropical rain forest lost in 1989 according to a recent estimate – many of these spiders will be extinct before we get around to finding them.

Two major sub-orders of spiders are recognized and distinguished by the arrangement of the fangs. In the Orthognatha, which includes the bird-eating and trapdoor spiders, the fangs strike downwards, like a pair of daggers working parallel with each other, but in the Labidognatha – which includes the great majority of spiders – the two fangs close together like a pair of pointed sugar tongs. Members of the Labidognatha are often called true spiders, but this is just confusing and a better name is araneomorph spiders. Members of the Orthognatha are commonly called mygalomorph spiders. A third sub-order, known as the Mesothelae, also has parallel fangs, but it contains just a few rather primitive spiders living in the Far East.

The arrangement of the breathing organs and the silk-producing organs, together with the arrangement of the eyes and the number of claws on the feet, are used to split the two main sub-orders into smaller family groups. About 90 families are recognized at present, but spider experts can't agree on the arrangement of the families and new schemes for classifying the spiders have appeared with alarming frequency during the last few decades.

Eurypelma mesomelas, *a typical mygalomorph or bird-eating spider.*

FROM THE OUTSIDE

There are podgy spiders and skinny spiders, short ones and lanky ones, and some that are as flat as pancakes, but, whatever their shape, all spiders come in two halves. These are technically known as the prosoma and the opisthosoma, but they are the head and the body to most people. Many readers will probably be happy to call them the front and rear halves, even though the opisthosoma – commonly known as the abdomen – is usually a good deal larger than the prosoma. The two regions are joined by a petite waist known as the pedicel. Like all arthropods, the spiders have a fairly tough outer skeleton, although it is not particularly hard and on the rear half of the body it is often quite soft. The skeleton contains a waxy layer, but it is not completely waterproof and most spiders die very quickly in dry air through losing water by evaporation.

The front half
The front half, which is also known as the cephalothorax because it is an amalgamation of the head and thorax, carries almost all the external working bits. It is covered by a tough shield called the carapace, which usually carries a pattern of grooves marking the positions of the muscles that work the legs and the stomach pump (see page 22).

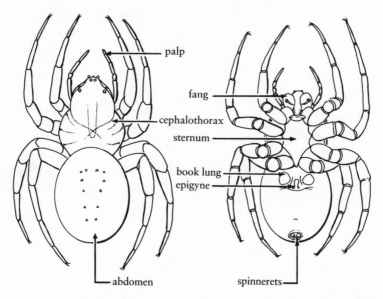

A spider from above (left) *and below, showing the main external features.*

The eyes are dotted around the front edge of the carapace, sometimes on an elevated platform. Most spiders have eight eyes, arranged in two or three rows, and each family has its own characteristic pattern. There are also plenty of six-eyed spiders, and some with only four or two eyes. Some cave-living species, in common with many other animals of the dark, have no eyes at all. Spider eyes are quite unlike the multi-lensed compound eyes of insects. Each one has a simple lens, formed from a transparent patch of the cuticle and overlying a bunch of nerve cells that form a simple retina. There is often a reflecting layer behind the retina. Known as the tapetum, it sends the light rays back through the retina, stimulating the nerve cells a second time and thus increasing the sensitivity of the eye. The tapetum is responsible for the gleam in a spider's eyes when it is picked out by torchlight.

But even spiders with eight eyes usually have poor sight, and they rely mainly on scents and vibrations to tell them what is happening in the world. The exceptions are some of the hunting spiders – especially the jumping spiders, whose big central eyes stare out like headlights (see page 46). Some jumping spiders can perceive sharp images of prey and other objects as much as 30cm (12 inches) away, but even jumping spiders' eyes are small beside those of the ogre-faced or gladiator spiders (see page 72). Up to about 1.5mm (0.06 inch) across, these are the largest simple eyes of any arthropod and, although they do not produce very clear images, their amazing ability to gather and concentrate light makes them fantastic for night work.

A spider's fangs have several uses, including digging burrows and carrying egg cocoons, but their primary function is for attack and defence. Although the longest fangs are only some 12mm (0.5 inch) long and most are very much shorter, their venom makes them into truly formidable weapons. Each fang is like a curved, hollow needle and it is attached to a basal segment which, in turn, is connected to the carapace just in front of the mouth. In the mygalomorphs – the bird-eaters and trapdoor spiders – the basal segments project horizontally from the carapace and the hinged fangs lie side by side beneath them. In the majority of spiders – the araneomorphs – the basal segments hang vertically and the fangs face each other like a pair of tongs or tweezers. The central canal of each fang is connected to the venom glands. Among the trapdoor spiders and their relatives the venom glands are contained entirely within the large basal segments, but in the other spiders the glands extend into the front half of the body. The basal segments are often toothed and are used to tear and crush the spiders' prey when it has been caught.

Just behind the fangs come the palps, officially known as pedipalps because they resemble the legs – although they are usually a good deal

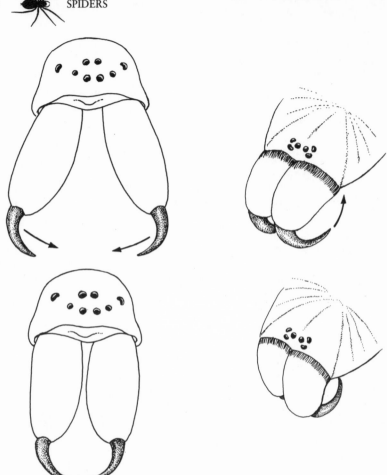

The fangs of the araneomorphs (left) *close together like tongs or tweezers, while those of the mygalomorph spiders* (right) *stab their victims like two parallel daggers.*

shorter than the legs. Each palp has six segments, the basal one of which is used, together with the basal segments of the fangs, for cutting and crushing the prey. In most spiders this segment is equipped with toothed ridges which act like tiny saws. The other segments of the palps function more like the antennae of insects. They are loaded with sense organs (see page 20) to detect scents and vibrations. The palps of male spiders are also used for signalling to the females and for fooling around with the females when they have got together. Their swollen tips, which make it easy to distinguish mums from dads, are used to impregnate the females (see page 87).

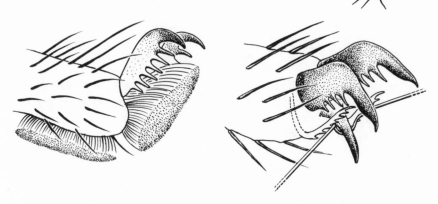

The foot of a hunting spider (left) *showing the adhesive hair tufts or scopulae, and the foot of an orb-web spider* (right) *showing the toothed claws and hairs with which it grips its web.*

The four pairs of walking legs all have seven segments. The front legs are usually the longest and they are used largely for exploring the surroundings and picking up signals. Each foot has two or three sharp claws. Hunting spiders, which make no webs, have just two comb-like claws on each foot, but web-spinning species have a third claw in the middle. These central claws are not toothed but, in conjunction with tufts of serrated bristles, they allow the spiders to maintain a secure grip on their silken threads (see above). The feet of many hunting spiders are provided with dense tufts of hair known as scopulae, and the hairs all have 'split-ends'. Each hair may split into several hundred filaments, known as end-feet, and under high magnification it looks like a tiny brush. The end-feet have spatulate tips, and physical adhesion between these tips and the substrate enables a properly equipped spider to climb window panes with ease. If, as happens pretty well everywhere in nature, there is a microscopic film of moisture on the substrate, the system works even better. The scopulae also help to hold the spiders' prey. Like the pedipalps, the legs are well supplied with sense organs for picking up scents and vibrations. They play a major role in finding and capturing prey as well as in the construction of webs.

Anyone who has tried to pick up spiders, or even brush them into a dustpan, must have noticed how they sometimes collapse with their legs in a tangle. This is the natural consequence of even a slight injury to any part of the body. The legs are full of flexor muscles, which bend each joint as required, but extension of the legs is brought about entirely by an increase in blood pressure caused by the pumping action of muscles in the prosoma – so any injury resulting in loss of blood renders the spider helpless.

The rear half

The rear half of the spider's body – the opisthosoma – is basically a soft bag with few obvious external features, although it is often brightly coloured and sometimes elegantly sculptured among the orb-web spiders. It is commonly egg-shaped, although often spherical and sometimes tubular. The only appendages on this part of the body are the spinnerets – sometimes simply called spinners – which spew out the silk, but even these are pretty well concealed in most spiders when they are not in use. Only in the house spiders and trapdoor spiders and a few other groups are the spinnerets really conspicuous. There are usually six of them, but they are not all the same size. The spinnerets and their functions are described in detail on page 26.

Sensitive bristles

Stick a spider under a magnifying glass and you can't fail to notice its assorted hairs and bristles. Some are much hairier than others and, although it is the hairiness that puts many people off spiders, hairs are important for spiders. Vibrations of one kind or another, including sounds, play a central role in a spider's life and virtually every part of its body is equipped to pick up and assess the vibrations that reach it. Long or short, thick or thin, all the hairs are connected to the spider's nervous system and they respond to a variety of vibrations and tactile signals that might signify food, enemies or mates.

In accordance with the modern proverb that today's scientists are discovering more and more about less and less, the best studied of the spiders' hairs are the very slender ones, called trichobothria, that occur on the outer parts of the palps and legs. Generally under a millimetre long, although most spiders have a few longer ones, these hairs sprout from cup-like sockets and, like blades of grass waving in the breeze, they are ruffled by the slightest air movement. So sensitive are they that some spiders can pick up the vibrations of flies crawling over 30cm (12 inches) away, and, because the nerve endings detect the direction in which the hairs bend, the spiders can even pin-point the positions of the flies pretty accurately.

A second kind of vibration-detector consists of a minute slit in the body wall. Called a slit sensilla, it is between 0.008mm and 0.2mm long and contains a nerve ending attached to a very thin membranous roof. A spider may have more than 3,000 slit sensillae and, as well as picking up vibrations, they act like strain gauges, detecting minute deformations of the body wall and telling the spider about the position of its legs and body. Slit sensillae may occur singly, but they are more often clustered together, especially on the legs. The clusters are called lyriform organs – because they are often shaped like an old-fashioned lyre – and within each one the

..."THEY'RE PLAYING OUR SONG!"

sensillae all run parallel to each other, although they are of varying lengths. Like the trichobothria, the lyriform organs pick up airborne sounds as well as other vibrations. This has been proved by recording the sounds of amorous male spiders (see page 84) and then serenading females with the recordings. The females definitely respond to the sounds.

Spiders also taste and smell with their feet and palps, which carry scores of taste-hairs. Unlike the tactile hairs, these are slightly curved and hollow. Numerous nerve endings are exposed at the tip of each hair and a brief contact is all that is necessary for them to assess the suitability of food. Male spiders also use their taste hairs to pick up female trails (see page 84). Scents, of which the most important to spiders are the pheromones used in courtship, are detected by hundreds of microscopic pores on the feet, each equipped with a sensitive nerve ending.

TO THE INSIDE

A diet of soup

Soup is always the dish of the day for the spider. Its mouth, hidden away between the fangs and the palps, is too small for solids, so a good deal of food preparation has to take place outside the body. The venom contains an assortment of powerful digestive enzymes and digestion of the prey starts the moment it is bitten. More digestive fluids flow from the mouth as the bases of the fangs and palps get to work to cut and crush the prey, and the meal is quickly reduced to a soggy lump. The stomach gets going like a suction pump as soon as digestion is under way. Strong muscles connect it to the walls of the carapace (see page 16), and when the muscles contract they stretch the stomach and the liquefied food gushes in. The indigestible bits, held back by bristles around the mouth, are discarded in a ball. Further filtering of the food takes place in the pharynx (gullet) on the way to the stomach. Rings of muscle then squeeze the stomach and force the liquid into the mid-gut, whose branching pouches occupy much of the rear half of the body and a good deal of the front half as well. They even extend into the legs. The mass of pouches is sometimes known as the liver. Digestion is completed here and the food is absorbed into the tissues.

Because the spider's food is liquefied before it enters the mouth, and contains no food particles more than about 0.001mm in diameter, there is very little solid waste, but what there is passes through a short hind gut and leaves the body through the anus in the form of small pellets, which are easily seen beneath the web of a house spider. Metabolic waste – from the tissues – also contributes to the pellets. It is absorbed from the blood and other tissues by a network of slender tubes (the Malpighian tubules) spreading through the rear half of the body and, in the form of crystals of uric acid and other insoluble materials, it passes into the hind gut.

Leaky blood systems

For its size, the spider is a big-hearted fellow. Lying in a cavity in the rear half of the body, the heart may be nearly half the length of the spider. It is a muscular, sausage-like tube with a number of slits that look like tiny button holes. Contraction of the heart forces the blood along narrow arteries to all parts of the body – a tight squeeze in the pedicel, which also has to carry the gut and the nerves controlling the activities of the spider's rear end. The blood, transparent blue instead of deep red like our own, leaks from the tips of the arteries and bathes all the tissues. It gradually finds its way back to

Spider insides – the internal structure of a female.

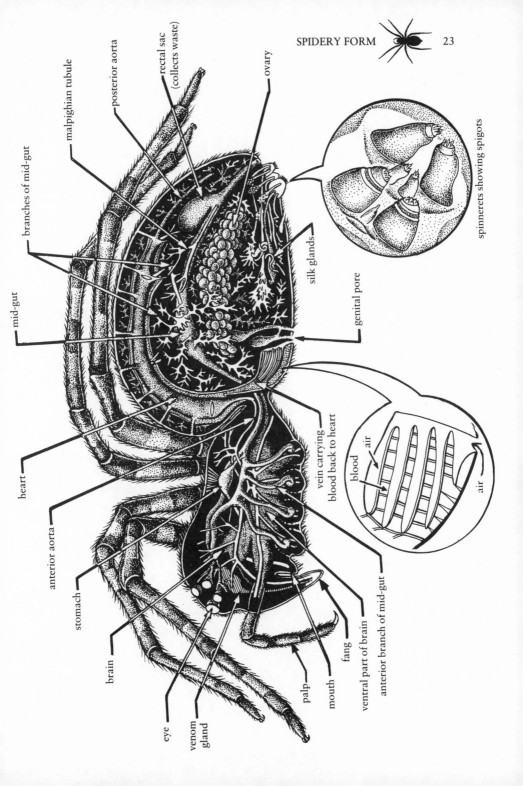

rectal sac
(collects waste)

posterior aorta

malpighian tubule

branches of mid-gut

ovary

spinnerets showing spigots

silk glands

mid-gut

genital pore

heart

vein carrying
blood back to heart

blood

air

air

anterior aorta

stomach

brain

anterior branch of mid-gut

ventral part of brain

mouth

fang

palp

eye

venom
gland

the cavity around the heart. When the heart relaxes, the 'button holes' open, allowing the blood back in for another journey round the body. This kind of circulation is known as an open circulation and is very common among invertebrates.

Two ways of breathing

Most spiders have two distinct sets of breathing apparatus – book-lungs and tracheae. Book-lungs are little pouches in the rear half of the body and they open to the air through narrow slits on the underside, usually just behind the pedicel. Inside each pouch the body is thrown into lots of thin folds which look like the pages of a book – hence the name. Blood flows through the pages, absorbing oxygen from the air in the pouch and carrying it round the body. The tracheae are slender tubes, usually much branched, that permeate the body and carry air to the tissues, just as they do in insects. They open to the outside through one or two minute pores called spiracles, usually just in front of the spinnerets. Tracheae are sometimes confined to the rear half of the body, but in many species they extend throughout the front half as well. Most spiders have one pair of book-lungs and one pair of tracheae, although the more primitive kinds, including the trapdoor spiders and their relatives, have two pairs of book-lungs and no tracheae. Some species, including the slow-moving daddy-long-legs spiders, make do with just one pair of book-lungs. Spiders with well developed tracheae often have smaller hearts than other species, because the blood is less concerned with carrying oxygen.

The silk glands and the reproductive organs, which occupy much of the lower half of the opisthosoma, are described in later sections.

Spider silk

A spider's life is literally wrapped up in silk right from the beginning, for all spider species protect their eggs by packing them in silken cocoons. And from the moment they leave their eggs, the spiders embark on a life of almost continuous silk production. They make several kinds of silk in various glands in the rear half of the body. The silks are all proteins belonging to a group called fibroins and they are quite similar to silkworm silk, but they lack the outer coating of sericin that gives silkworm silk its characteristic shine.

A few mygalomorph spiders produce only one or two kinds of silk, but most spiders are a good deal more versatile and most individuals possess between three and six different kinds of silk glands. Each one produces a different kind of silk and each kind of silk has a different purpose. The orb-web spiders and their relatives have the most silk glands, for only these produce a viscid silk or glue, and females always have one more than their mates because they need a special silk for wrapping their eggs. Each set of glands is connected by long ducts to one or more spinnerets. The major silk glands and the main functions of their silk are listed in the following table.

The spider's silk glands

Gland	Function of silk	Spinneret
Pyriform	Attachment discs for webs and life-lines	Anterior
Ampullate	Frame threads of web; drag-lines and life-lines; ballooning	Anterior and middle
Aciniform	Prey-wrapping; outer wall of egg cocoon	Middle and posterior
Tubuliform (female only)	Inner layers of egg cocoon	Middle and posterior
Aggregate*	Glue for sticky threads	Posterior
Flagelliform*	Spiral thread of orb-web and catching threads of some other spiders	Posterior
Cribellate†	Hackle-bands	Cribellum

* Found only in orb-web spiders and theridiid spiders
† Found only in cribellate spiders (see page 28)

Spewing out the silk

Most spiders have three pairs of spinnerets. These are small and inconspicuous in many species, including the orb-web spiders, but they are sometimes long and jointed and they waggle about like little fingers. Each spinneret has a number of fine tubes or spigots at its tip, and these are the actual openings of the silk glands. The smallest tubes, sometimes called spools, are crowded together in one area and, among other things, they produce the broad bands of silk with which the spiders wrap their prey. The larger spigots are scattered all over the tips of the spinnerets, although there are rarely more than half a dozen spigots on each one. They are of several different shapes and sizes and their muscular valves can be adjusted to alter the thickness of the extruded silk. They normally produce coarser strands than the spools. Some spiders have an extra spinning organ, called the cribellum, just in front of the spinnerets. This is a small plate carrying hundreds or even thousands of minute spigots which spew out the finest of all silks from their own special glands.

The silk glands have no muscles around them and the silk, which starts off as a syrupy liquid, cannot be pumped out. The spider may be able to start the flow by increasing the blood pressure around the glands, but after that the silk has to be pulled out – usually by the legs. This action is most clearly seen when a spider is wrapping its prey in a broad bandage of silk. The pulling is an essential part of the spinning process, for it is the stretching of the long silk molecules that causes them to bond together and solidify into strands. Contrary to popular opinion, it is not contact with the air that causes the silk to harden. Spiders can spin two or more kinds of silk at the same time, pulling them from different spigots and deftly manipulating them with their legs and spinnerets. Each gland is permanently connected to its spigots, so the spider has no worries about connecting up the right bits. All it has to do is to follow its instincts and use the right silk for the right job.

Strong and stretchy

The silk strand emerging from an individual spigot may be as little as 0.000015mm in diameter, although it is normal for several strands to coalesce to form a functional thread. The drag-line of the garden spider, for example, has a diameter in the region of 0.003mm. When dealing with such slender threads it is often more convenient to use denier measurements, the denier of a given thread being the weight in grams of a 9-kilometre length. Human hair averages about 50 denier. Silkworm silk is about one denier, meaning that a 9-kilometre length weighs just one gram, but the drag-line silk of the garden spider is a mere 0.07 denier. A strand of this silk long enough to encircle the earth – about 40,000km (25,000 miles) – would

weigh only 340g (12oz).

Incredibly thin it may be, but spider silk is still extremely strong. In fact, it is the strongest of all natural fibres. Some spider silks are stronger than steel strands of equivalent thickness and very nearly as strong as nylon. The drag-line of the garden spider can support about half a gram without snapping, but a steel strand of similar thickness will snap when loaded with only a quarter of a gram. The tenacity of spider silk varies with its function. Cocoon silk, for example, does not have to support any weight and is relatively weak.

Spider silk is also amazingly elastic, as you can see if you watch the behaviour of an orb-web in a breeze. The frame threads and radii are continually stretching and contracting as the twigs to which they are attached sway backwards and forwards. They can increase their length by about a third without snapping, but they are by no means the most elastic of silks: the threads of the gladiator spider's web (see page 74) can increase their lengths sixfold. A steel thread, by contrast, can increase by only about 8 per cent of its original length before breaking.

Sticking without glue

The orb-webs made by the garden spider and its relatives in the family Araneidae catch prey with the aid of a viscid kind of silk secreted by the aggregate glands and applied to the spiral thread as it leaves the spinnerets. But there are other webs that are even more sticky, and yet they have no glue at all. These are made by the cribellate spiders and their secret lies in the incredibly fine, bluish silk produced by the cribellum. The cribellate spider produces perfectly normal strands of silk from its spinnerets and then covers them with the cribellum silk, which is brushed from the cribellum by a compact patch of bristles, called the calamistrum, on each hind leg. Each bristle carries several rows of microscopic teeth and acts like a minute hair brush. The cribellum silk forms ribbons but, because the legs vibrate rapidly while brushing, the individual threads – only about 0.000015mm in diameter – are thrown into microscopic loops. And here is the catch! Any insect unfortunate enough to touch the ribbons quickly gets its feet entangled in the loops and is held fast – without any glue. Silk of this kind is called calamistrated silk, and the glueless ribbons are called hackle-bands. They remain effective much longer than the glue-studded threads of the garden spider, which gather dust and dry out within a few days. They even work after several months in a warm oven, but do not last for ever. Dust gradually builds up between the threads, and rain causes them to mat together, just as water causes cotton wool to collapse, so the spider has to spin fresh threads from time to time. Calamistrated webs are produced by a wide variety of spiders, including *Amaurobius* (page 81) and *Uloborus* (page 67).

Freshly made calamistrated silk even sticks firmly to glass, but there is one puzzling problem: if the hackle-bands are so good at trapping things, why do their makers not get trapped themselves?

Web-beginnings

The earliest spiders were undoubtedly hunters. We don't know when they began to make webs, but scattered fossils show us that spiders living in the coal forests some 300 million years ago already had well developed spinnerets. Even if they were not making decent webs, they had certainly been making silk for a while. Silk was probably used from the beginning for making simple shelters and for protecting the eggs, and prey-catching webs must have evolved from the jumble of drag-lines surrounding the shelters. Insects stumbling into the silk may not have become trapped, but they would certainly have alerted the spiders to their presence. The untidiest spiders probably did quite well for food and, freed from the need to go hunting, they had more time and energy for reproduction and they reared

plenty of untidy offspring to carry on the trend. Many refinements were necessary to produce today's wide range of exquisite web designs, but remember that the spiders have had getting on for 400 million years in which to experiment.

The early web-builders probably relied on crawling insects for food, and it is quite possible that the presence of so many spiders actually stimulated the evolution of wings and flight in insects. Having got themselves airborne, the insects were relatively safe from spider attack, but evolution does not stand still and natural selection favoured those spiders leaving strands of silk on vegetation. These strands would have brought down the occasional insect, so the scene was set for the evolution of the wide range of aerial webs (those suspended in the air) that we see today.

Silk recycling

Many web-spinning spiders simply add more silk to their webs from time to time, often ending up with the scruffy accumulations of silk that we see in the corners of outhouses or draped over low-growing vegetation. The garden spider and other orb-web spiders display a bit more breeding and many of them renew their webs every day – or, to be more accurate, every night. Although the web itself is very light – that of an average garden spider contains 20–30 yards of silk and weighs well under 0.5mg – its production represents a considerable investment of energy and materials and the spider seems to be aware of this. The old silk is rolled up, rapidly liquefied with digestive juices, and then slurped up like any other food. Investigations with radioactive tracers show that almost all the silk proteins ingested by the garden spider end up in its ampullate glands, from where they emerge again to form new radii and frame threads and the all-important drag-lines. The recycling is very quick, but we do not yet know the route that the silk proteins take to the ampullate glands.

Can we use spider silk?

If spider silk is so strong, why don't we make use of it ourselves? A Frenchman named Bon – obviously a good chap as well as a very patient one – showed that spider silk certainly *can* be used in the same way as silkworm silk, for he made some gloves and even some stockings from it early in the 18th century, but commercial use of spider silk is just not practical. The silk is too fine to stand up to machine spinning and weaving, and even if this problem could be solved, think of the enormous number of spiders needed for a commercial operation. Another Frenchman, René Réaumur, estimated that 663,552 spiders (he did not say which kind) would have to be collected and 'milked' to obtain a single pound of silk! And then remember that spiders are predatory creatures and would have to be housed separately and served with regular helpings of live flies! It's just not on. But we do use spider silk for some things. The cross-wires used to divide up the field of view in optical gadgets are often made from the fine silk of the black widow spider, while at the other end of the scale the webs of the golden orb-web spiders (*Nephila* spp) are used as fishing nets in some tropical areas. *Nephila* silk is the strongest of all natural fibres and is certainly the best candidate for commercial use. More than 700 metres of silk can be pulled from one of these spiders, and the silk has been used to make cloth for tapestry work.

Spider venom

With the exception of members of the family Uloboridae, all spiders use venom for killing or paralysing their prey. The venom is secreted by the cells of a pair of venom glands and carried to the fangs by narrow ducts. The glands are cylindrical, and among the mygalomorph spiders – the bird-eaters and trapdoor spiders – they are contained entirely within the basal segments of the fangs or chelicerae. In all other spiders – the araneomorphs – the venom glands extend well back into the prosoma, but this does not mean that these spiders have larger venom glands than the mygalomorphs. The chelicerae of the mygalomorphs are considerably larger than the entire bodies of many other spiders and can accommodate venom glands up to 12mm (0.5 inch) in length and 1.5mm in diameter. This compares with a length of 2mm (0.08 inch) and a diameter of about 0.3mm (0.01 inch) for the venom glands of the notorious black widow. Nevertheless, the largest of all venom glands do belong to an araneomorph spider: the South American *Phoneutria nigriventer* manages to pack in a pair of glands up to 10mm (0.4 inch) long and 2.7mm (0.1 inch) in diameter. These glands can hold up to 8mg of one of the most toxic of all spider venoms.

Bands of powerful muscle spiral around the glands, and when these muscles contract, the venom is pumped out through the fangs with great force. The largest fangs belong, not surprisingly, to the big mygalomorph spiders. Those of *Theraphosa leblondi* are up to 12mm (0.5 inch) long and those of many other bird-eating spiders exceed 8mm (0.3 inch). *Phoneutria nigriventer*, the largest of South America's araneomorph spiders, has fangs about 4.5mm (0.18 inch) long, while the black widow's fangs are a paltry 0.4mm (0.016 inch) long. But fang length bears little relationship to the seriousness of a spider's bite: the nature of the venom is much more important and the little fangs of the black widow can inflict far more damage on us than the massive daggers of the bird-eating spiders. The barbed hairs of the bird-eating spiders are often more damaging than their venom, for they can work themselves deep into the flesh and set up distressing irritation and infection.

Spider venoms started out purely as digestive juices, but gradually evolved into complex mixtures of toxic proteins and flesh-destroying enzymes, manufactured in different regions of the venom glands and by different kinds of cells. Their exact composition varies from species to species. The venoms are lethal to insects and some other small animals, but only about 30 of the 40,000 or so known spider species are at all dangerous to people – and few of these attack unless provoked. Most of the dangerous species are actually quite small. The black widow, for example, is no more than about 15mm (0.6 inch) long. Most bites are received when the spiders are trapped in clothing or inadvertently picked up with vegetation or other materials. About a fifth of the patients treated for black widow bites over a period of years at a Croatian medical centre had been bitten on the left forearm – the part of the arm used to hold sheaves of wheat while they are being cut and bound (see page 79).

The venom of the black widow has four main toxic ingredients, three of which are aimed primarily at the spider's insect prey. The fourth component is the nerve poison that causes so much trouble when the spider bites someone. The bite is not usually noticed at first – *Latrodectus*, the spider's generic name, actually means 'secret biter' – but severe pains begin within about 15 minutes. They usually start in the lymph nodes of the groin or arm-pit, depending on where the bite is received, and then spread to the abdomen and other parts of the body. The muscles tighten up and breathing becomes very difficult. Furious sweating and nausea normally accompany the pain. Although many deaths have been recorded over the centuries, especially in young children and the elderly, most people recover from black widow bites after a few days, and now that antivenins are available to treat the widows' victims, deaths are very rare.

The venom of the American black widow is thought to be about 15 times more poisonous than the same quantity of rattlesnake venom, although the spider obviously injects a much smaller amount of venom than a rattlesnake. Black widows living in other parts of the world, including southern Europe and Australasia, are generally considered to be less venomous than the American black widow, but they are still pretty nasty and can certainly kill people.

In addition to the paralysing nerve poisons that occur in the venoms of most of the dangerous spiders, there are several tissue-destroying poisons. The venoms of the brown recluse spider (*Loxosceles reclusa*) and its relatives in the Americas damage blood and other tissues and can cause serious damage to the liver and kidneys, although it is only in recent decades that these spiders have been recognized as medically important. Wolf spiders, including the true tarantula, also have tissue-destroying (cytotoxic) venoms, but with the exception of a few large species from tropical America their effects are usually local and of short duration. The Australian white-tailed spider (*Lampona cylindrata*), which is not uncommon on the walls of sheds and houses, feeds mainly on other spiders, but has recently been accused of biting people and causing some very unpleasant wounds that take a long time to heal. Its venom obviously contains a cytotoxic element, and the fact that it has only recently been accused of wrong-doing suggests

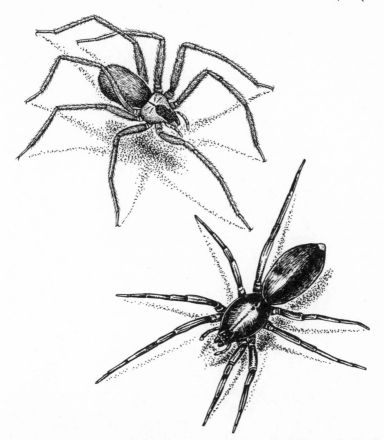

The American brown recluse spider (top) *and the Australian white-tailed spider are both about a centimetre long.*

that it may have only recently acquired the poison through some kind of genetic mutation. Many spider venoms also contain histamine, which may be responsible for much of the initial pain of a bite.

Powerful nerve poisons and blood-destroying agents are not necessary for killing prey and it is difficult to explain why spiders possess such awesome ammunition. Perhaps it is just an accident of nature that has made a handful of spiders into such dangerous adversaries. But whatever the reason, Kipling was certainly right about spiders: the female of the species *is* more deadly than the male. Male spiders, being generally smaller than the females, have less venom and smaller fangs. No male spider is capable of killing an adult human.

TARANTULAS, DANCES AND BLACK WIDOWS

The legendary tarantula of southern Europe is a large wolf spider, named for its association with the Italian town of Taranto. Its painful bite was supposed to be fatal unless the victims flung themselves around in bouts of furious dancing until they dropped from exhaustion. During the Middle Ages, musicians began to play for the dancing, and both the dance and the music became known as the tarantella. Onlookers frequently took up the frenzied dance and became enveloped in a kind of mass hysteria, called tarantism, that swept through whole communities. Strange as it might seem, there was some truth in the idea that dancing would help to rid the victim of the pain, for a high temperature and consequent dilation of the blood vessels does help to dissipate and drive out the poison. But what the people did not know was that they were dancing for the wrong spider! The bite of the tarantula (*Lycosa narbonensis*) is not serious and causes only transient pain. The real

The true tarantula, wrongly accused of causing trouble.

culprit was the European black widow (*Latrodectus tredecimguttatus*). This spider was known to the Ancient Greeks and Romans, several of whom described the effects of its bite and the restless movements of victims searching for relief from the pain. Somewhere in the dim recesses of history the saga became associated with the tarantula. Tarantella dancing is still popular in Italy – and it could be said that tarantism is still alive and kicking in some holiday resorts – but this way of treating spider bites has died out with the advent of antivenins.

Making antivenins

Antivenins, also known as anti-toxins or anti-sera, are now available for treating victims of almost all the dangerous spiders, including black widows, funnel-webs, *Phoneutria*, *Loxosceles* and the South American wolf spiders. The starting point for the antivenins is the venom itself, which is usually extracted from the spiders by giving them mild electric shocks. This causes the muscles around the venom glands to contract and fire out the venom. Large spiders can also be 'milked' by squeezing them gently with forceps. The venom, which is a clear, transparent liquid, is collected and injected in carefully measured doses into horses or rabbits. The animals gradually build up an immunity in the form of antibodies, and by bleeding the animals from time to time the antibodies can be obtained and purified for use as antivenins. The spiders themselves can be 'milked' every two or three weeks.

A NEW USE FOR VENOMS?

Because spider venoms are targeted primarily at their insect prey, research is going on to find ways of manufacturing their paralysing nerve poisons artificially. This could lead to the development of a new generation of environmentally friendly insecticides with no harmful residues. Because the poisons are destroyed in the digestive system, birds would not be harmed by eating the paralysed insects.

Finding food

THE HUNTERS

Although the web-spinning species are the most familiar of the spiders, only about half of the world's spiders spin webs to trap their prey. The rest go in search of food, just as their early ancestors did, or else lie in wait to ambush passing animals. So hunting, trapping and ambushing are the three main ways for spiders to get their food but, as we shall see, the dividing lines often get a bit blurred. There are ambushers that use silk to alert them to the approach of prey, and then run out to catch it – and thus could be accused of hunting. And there are hunters and ambushers that could be accused of trapping because they throw silk at their prey to restrain it. But let's stick to the dictionary, so the hunters are those that roam freely in search of prey – using various combinations of stealth, speed, strength and agility to capture their victims. They include some of the world's most dangerous spiders (see page 44). In some parts of South America hunting spiders are believed to kill more people than poisonous snakes.

Prowling monsters
The big, shaggy bird-eating spiders, belonging to the family Theraphosidae, all live by hunting. They are called baboon spiders in Africa, but most people, especially in America, insist on calling them tarantulas. This name really belongs to a European wolf spider (see page 43), but the name has stuck so firmly to the bird-eaters that it is unlikely to be dislodged. Even bird-eater is not a particularly good name. Some of the 300 or so species do occasionally eat birds, but most of them feed on insects. They all live in tropical and sub-tropical areas and they include the largest of all spiders – with bodies up to 12.5cm (5 inches) long and legs spanning some 25cm (10 inches). With weights up to about 85g (3oz), they are among the heaviest of all land-living arthropods.

The theraphosids prowl around at night, on the ground or in the trees, and sink their fangs into anything they find. Like all spiders, they trail silk behind them and they are undoubtedly aware of anything that bumps into the silken trails. They also detect prey by scent and by picking up vibrations with their sensitive hairs, and then run it down with a quick sprint. Although these spiders feed mainly on insects, some of them prefer lizards and frogs, and even kill poisonous snakes on occasion. The birds that they eat are usually chicks in their nests or hen birds sitting on eggs. Despite their huge fangs, the theraphosids are fairly placid creatures and unlikely to bite people unless they are handled roughly. With a few exceptions, their venoms have no lasting effect on people, although they can produce severe pain for a short while. Infection of the deep wounds is often more serious than the actual venoms, and the spiders' hairs can also be quite troublesome (see page 106).

The woodlouse specialist

Spiders are not usually very fussy about their food and, although they quickly dump various bugs and other insects with disagreeable tastes, most of them eat just about any animal they can catch. But there are some specialist assassins, dealing with particular groups of prey, such as ants, and sometimes with just one particular species. Species of *Dysdera* specialize in catching and eating woodlice, whose tough armour and repellent glands make them unattractive to most spiders. *Dysdera crocata* is a rather ponderous, short-sighted, six-eyed spider that lurks under logs and stones by day and emerges to hunt at night. Guided mainly by scent and a bit of luck, it bumps into the occasional woodlouse, and then its monstrous fangs come into play. Long basal segments give the fangs a yawning gape and, by tilting its front end to one side, the spider can sink one fang into the back of the woodlouse and the other into its belly. *D. crocata* is one of several species with a chestnut brown carapace and a flesh-coloured rear. It is a

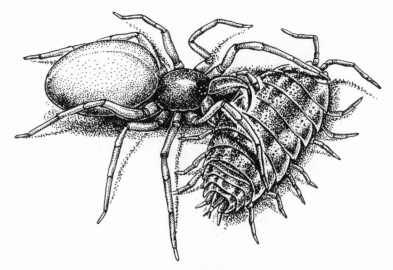

Huge fangs enable Dysdera crocata, *about 12mm long, to pierce the tough armour of a woodlouse.*

cosmopolitan creature found in and around human settlements in many parts of the world, probably through stowing away in produce of various kinds. It is one of only about twelve spider species living in the British Isles that are capable of inflicting a painful bite on a human.

The silk-throwers

The little spiders of the widespread genus *Euryopis* could well have been called the gladiators of the spider world, had not this name already been given to the web-throwing ogre-faced spiders (see page 72). Although *Euryopis* species belong to the same family as the black widow and other scaffold-web spiders (see page 76), they make no webs and for a long time were thought to be honest hunters, but recent investigations, particularly those of J.E. Carico with *E. funebris* in North America, have shown that these spiders do, in fact, make use of silk for prey capture. Some of them hunt on the ground, but *funebris* prefers to hunt in the shrub layer and spends its evenings scuttling up and down the branches in search of ants, which seem to be its only prey. As soon as it meets an ant, the spider does a quick about-face and uses its back legs to fling a few loops of gum-laden silk over the unfortunate insect. Only then, with the ant stuck to the twig, does the spider move in and bite one of its legs. The victim is then fixed to the spider's spinnerets and carted away. It may be eaten in a convenient crevice, but more often the spider takes its meal while dangling from a short life-line.

Compared with the web-making members of its family, *Euryopis* is very economical in its use of silk, but such thriftiness can pay off only if the spider can be sure of getting itself among the ants in the first place. It is likely that the spider achieves this by picking up the scent of the ants and confining its activities only to the branches on which the ants normally forage.

Drassodes species are ruthless, ground-living fighters whose speed and agility enable them to tackle a wide range of prey. They are more than a match for most other spiders, including species considerably larger than themselves. They hunt at night and find their prey by scent and touch. Like *Euryopis*, *Drassodes* deploys its silk only when a victim has been lined up, but its technique is quite different. A quick dab of the spinnerets fixes the silk to whatever the prey is standing on and then the spider darts round its opponent at high speed, securing it with a broad bandage of silk before leaping on to its back and delivering the fatal bite. The fight may be over in less than a second, even when the opponent is another large spider. *Drassodes lapidosus*, up to 15mm (0.6 inch) long with mouse-coloured fur, is a very common British species, often found under logs and in garden sheds.

Drassodes *immobilizes its prey with a broad bandage of silk.*

Spitting spiders

The little spitting spider of the family Scytodidae can usually be recognized by the much-enlarged front half of the body – the prosoma. In this spider this bulbous region is often noticeably larger than the rear half of the body, especially when the spider is hungry. Spitting spiders are very slow-moving, nocturnal creatures, and on first meeting them it is difficult to see how they can catch agile flies. But they are not called spitting spiders for nothing! They nail their victims by spitting venom at them from the two massive venom glands that occupy almost all of the enlarged cephalothorax. The spitting spiders' remarkable technique, unknown in any other group of spiders, was first fully described by Bristowe. Guided by vibrations, the spider creeps slowly towards its intended victim until it is within about a centimetre (0.5 inch) – the exact distance depends on the species – and then fires its venom glands. The fangs vibrate rapidly from side to side during firing and the victim finds itself pinned down by two zig-zag strands of quick-setting glue. This glue comes from the rear portion of each venom gland, and before bursting from the fangs it picks up a coating of paralysing venom from the front part of the gland. Spitting is used for defence against other spiders as well as for catching prey.

Most of the fifty or so species of spitting spiders live in tropical regions,

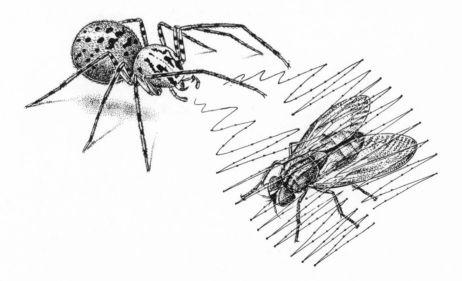

The yellow and black spitting spider (Scytodes thoracica) *pins down its victim with a set of well aimed, sticky and poisonous threads.*

but *Scytodes thoracica* occurs in and around buildings in all but the coldest parts of the world. It is quite common in southern Britain although, being no more than about 8mm (0.3 inch) long, it is not easy to find. It favours old houses that do not get too hot – it does not care for central heating – and prowls around the walls and ceilings at night. A good time to look for it is first thing in the morning, before opening the curtains. It spends the daytime in minute crevices around doors and window frames. The spider can live for about three years and, like many other spiders, can go without food for several months, during which time the rear half of its body shrinks to a fraction of its normal size.

Nippy wolf spiders

The wolf spiders of the family Lycosidae got their name because many of them chase after prey like wolves, although they are not social creatures and certainly do not hunt in packs. Their body lengths range from about 4mm to 30mm (0.16 to 1.2 inches). The hind legs are usually noticeably longer than the others. There are over 2,500 known species, scattered all over the world, although they are most numerous in the northern hemisphere. They make up a high proportion of the spiders in the far north and at high altitudes. Essentially ground-living, the wolf spiders are mostly drab brown or grey and well camouflaged in their natural habitats. Many species hunt among the fallen leaves on the forest floor, but others prefer open habitats, including seashores and heathland. *Pardosa groenlandica* abounds on the tundra of Greenland and North America, while *P. amentata* flourishes in gardens all over the northern hemisphere. *Pirata* species live in damp places and can even walk on water.

The family includes both diurnal and nocturnal species, with the diurnal ones most frequent in the cooler areas. *Pardosa amentata*, for example, enjoys basking on garden paths and rockeries. Juveniles are particularly fond of sunbathing and often assume a strange posture with the front four legs tucked up under the head almost like a pillow.

Wolf spiders have two large forward-facing eyes, two more looking to the sides, and four smaller ones in a row along the bottom of the face. By spider standards, their eyesight is pretty good (though this only means several centimetres!), although not as good as that of the jumping spiders. Movements detected by the eyes nearly always trigger the chase, although vibrations are important for many nocturnal species and particularly for those living and hunting in leaf litter. The chase often starts slowly to save energy, and some species rarely break into a trot, but for many species it ends with the spider hurling itself on to its victim after a high-speed dash. The fangs then do their work, usually digging into the victim's thorax, and

The European tarantula is a burrow-dwelling wolf spider up to about 25mm long.

the prey is consumed on the spot or taken back to the spider's lair. The powerful digestive juices can liquefy small prey within minutes. Springtails are the main prey of the smaller wolf spiders, but flies, beetles, grasshoppers and other spiders are regularly eaten by the larger species. The prey is often larger than the spider, but the wolf spider's powerful legs hold it firmly with the aid of their well developed scopulae (see page 19). The erectile spines on the spider's legs also help to keep the prey at a distance until the spider can deliver its paralysing bite. Wolf spiders living in vegetation some way above the ground often wrap their victims in silk, but the ground-living species never seem to bother with such measures.

Pardosa species are nomadic but many other wolf spiders, especially the larger species, make silk-lined burrows in the ground to which they return after each hunting excursion. Some species rarely move far from their burrows and make just short dashes to snatch up passing quarry, thus bridging the gap between the true hunters and the ambushers. A few species, including the European *Aulonia albimana*, still retain the ancestral web-making habit and produce small prey-catching webs similar to those of *Agelena* and the house spiders.

The tarantula of the Mediterranean region is among the largest of the wolf spiders, and certainly the most famous. This is the true tarantula, not to be confused with the hairy mygalomorphs that have acquired the same name (see page 37). The tarantula lives in a burrow and darts out to catch passing prey. It can inflict a painful bite if molested but, despite the legends surrounding it (see page 34), it is not a dangerous spider. Unfortunately, the same cannot be said of South America's wandering spiders, recently trans-

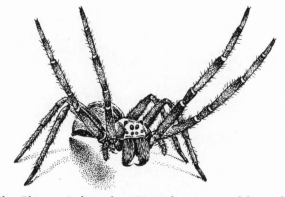

The Brazilian Phoneutria fera, *about 30mm long, is one of the world's most dangerous spiders.*

ferred to the Lycosidae from the Ctenidae. *Phoneutria fera*, one of the deadliest spiders, with fangs over 4mm (0.15 inch) long, often wanders into houses and is reputed to have killed two Brazilian children in one night when it got into their bed. It occasionally takes its wandering habit too far and turns up in Europe and elsewhere in consignments of bananas, and it can survive for some time in heated buildings.

Jumping jewels

The eyes of a hawk, the stealth of a cat and the finery of a parrot – that just about sums up the little jumping spiders, although a trip to one of the warmer parts of the world is necessary to see the most colourful of this family's jewels. Jumping spider watchers in the temperate regions generally have to be content with little brown or grey jobs, although even these are not lacking in charm.

Jumping spiders belong to the largest of all spider families – the Salticidae. There are about 4,000 known species and most of them live in the tropical regions. Very few are more than about 15mm (0.6 inch) long, but they exist in a bewildering variety of shapes. Some, like the various species of *Holoplatys*, are as flat as leaves and live under loose bark and between fence timbers. The body is clothed with flattened hairs, which are often brightly coloured and even iridescent – and led Alfred Wallace to describe the animals as 'more like jewels than spiders'. The males, which are usually smaller and more colourful than the females, display their colours in their spectacular courtship dances (see page 87).

None of the jumping spiders is dangerous to people and even the largest species would have to be very annoyed to bite anyone. Jumping spiders seem to be less frightening than most other spiders, perhaps because they have relatively short legs. Even the most ardent spider-hater can be enthralled by the colours of a jumping spider, and amused by its jaunty walk. Curiosity is another endearing feature – if any spider can be said to be endearing! The big eyes often stare back poker-faced as you approach, or perhaps the spider will dart away and then return almost immediately for another gawp. The spiders are essentially solitary creatures, but they sometimes gather to bask in sunny spots. Exploring the ruins of Filipi in northern Greece, I well remember wondering what the red spots were on the bases of some of the pillars. Moving closer, I found dozens of male *Philaeus chrysops* sunning themselves on the masonry. There were several on each pillar and when I got within about a couple of feet of a pillar they all sprinted to the far side, but after a few seconds their curiosity got the better of them and they returned to peer at me from the edges of the pillar.

Jumping spiders live and hunt mainly on rocks and tree trunks – and their man-made equivalents in the form of walls and fences – but many live on the ground or amongst the vegetation. One of the best known species is the well named zebra spider (*Salticus scenicus*), which is a familiar sight on rocks and walls all over the northern hemisphere.

The zebra spider, about 6mm long.

BLACK ZEBRAS

The zebra spider is very common in towns, where its favourite habitats are lichen-clad garden walls, gravestones and fences. The spider's normal pattern of black and white stripes camouflages it well when it sits still and gives it plenty of protection against birds in such situations, but in some industrial areas of northern England the spider has evolved an almost black form. The same thing has happened with many moths, and the accepted explanation here is that the black coloration, known as industrial melanism, protects the animals on smoke-blackened surfaces.

Jumping spiders are about in the daytime and are good runners, especially in bright sunshine, but they are obviously best known – and named – for their leaping abilities. Some species can leap more than forty times the length of their own bodies. Propulsion is provided by the fourth pair of legs, and sometimes by the third pair as well, although neither pair has any obvious modification for jumping. A sudden increase in blood pressure in the legs causes them to extend and send the spider hurtling forward – but not before it has anchored itself securely with a life-line like a skilled mountaineer. The amazing adhesion provided by the scopulae on its feet (see page 19) enables the jumping spider to hunt on vertical surfaces just as easily as on the flat.

Superb eyesight is the basis of the jumping spider's hunting strategy. There are eight eyes in three rows, with the two biggest ones in the middle of the front row. These are known as the anterior median or AM eyes – although they work just as well after lunch – and they are actually larger than the spider's brain! It is these eyes that glare at you when you challenge one of these spiders. They appear black when staring straight at you, but if they look pale the spider has its beady eyes on something else. Behind their big lenses, these eyes have a tubular construction with extra lenses and several retinal layers and they act almost like telescopes, producing clear images of small objects at various distances.

The other eyes are concerned mainly with detecting movement and, perched on the corners of the carapace, they give the spider almost 360° vision. The pedicel is very flexible, and the spider quickly swivels its front end around to focus on any movement with its main eyes. The whole body then swings into line ready for the cat-like stalk. The front lenses of the main eyes are fixed, but the rest of the eye tube can rotate to follow the movements of the prey, and each eye can move independently. No other

group of spiders can focus and judge distances as well as the jumpers. Their colour vision is also very good – why else would the spiders have such brilliant colours?

Focusing on a potential victim from as much as 30cm (1 foot) away, the spider moves slowly forward, not forgetting to secure its all-important life-line or drag-line at intervals. When it gets within 2–3cm (1 inch) of its quarry the spider launches itself forward and, with luck, its sturdy front legs pin the victim to the surface so that the fangs can get to work. Jumping spiders have even been seen leaping into the air to catch flying insects. Safely anchored by their life-lines, the spiders cannot fall very far, even when leaping from vertical surfaces, but the spiders' remarkable eyesight and co-ordination and the adhesive power of their scopulae ensure that falls are not common. The prey is not wrapped and is usually eaten on the spot, but may be taken to the silk-lined retreat that the spider uses at night.

Insects are the main victims of the jumping spiders, but a few jumpers have taken to stalking other spiders in their webs. Like the pirate spiders (see page 102), they entice their victims within range by vibrating the webs with their legs or palps and then pounce.

An aquatic hunter

Several kinds of spiders, including some wolf spiders, hunt in and around fresh water, but only one spider has learned how to live permanently under the water. This is the European water spider (*Argyroneta aquatica*), which

The European water spider, seen here with its air-filled home, is about 12mm long.

inhabits ponds and slow-moving streams all over the temperate regions of Eurasia. It belongs to the same family as the house spiders – the Agelenidae – and it spins a perfectly good sheet web in the water, but this web is not for catching prey: it will be the spider's home. With its slightly domed web firmly anchored to the vegetation, the spider nips up to the surface and grabs a bubble of air between the back legs and the body. The bubble is released under the sheet, causing it to bulge a bit more, and the spider goes up for another bubble. After several such operations, the sheet is converted into an air-filled dome or bell and is ready for occupation.

Although it sets up home under the water, the spider might just as well be living in the air and it has no obvious anatomical or physiological adaptations for underwater life. While away from its home, it obtains oxygen from the film of air trapped around its body by its hairy coat. The oxygen in the dome is gradually used up, although not as quickly as one might imagine. As the oxygen concentration falls, more diffuses in from the surrounding water, so the dome actually supplies more than the amount of oxygen originally brought from the surface. But the supply does need renewing occasionally, and when this happens the spider simply goes up and collects a few more bubbles.

The spider spends much of the daytime resting in the dome with just its front legs sticking out. These pick up the vibrations of passing animals and the spider streaks out to investigate. The spider can also detect insects struggling on the water surface. At night the water spider makes longer hunting expeditions, but it always returns to its air-filled home to enjoy its meals – guided by the silk strands that it trails behind it wherever it goes. The water would dilute the digestive enzymes poured on to the prey if the spider tried to dine in the water.

Fishing spiders

Spiders of the genus *Dolomedes* live in watery places, especially in swamps and marshes, and are known as fishing spiders or raft spiders. They belong to the family Pisauridae and are quite closely related to the wolf spiders, although they have longer and more pointed bodies – up to about 40mm (1.6 inches) long – and longer legs. They also have smaller eyes than the wolf spiders, in connection with their different hunting habits – which are on the borderline between ambushing and hunting. Some float freely on the water, but most species sit on floating leaves or other objects with their front legs resting lightly on the surface. Ripples on the surface herald the arrival of prey, and by detecting the direction of the ripples and the intervals between them, the spiders can pinpoint the position of the prey pretty accurately before skating out to grab it. The spiders catch small fishes and

The fishing spider relies on vibrations to inform it of approaching prey.

other creatures in the water as well as insects on the surface, and frequently dabble their front legs in the water to attract fishes. They can cope with prey up to twice the length of their own bodies. The eyes play virtually no part in the detection of prey: perched high on the carapace, they look up rather than forward, and certainly cannot spot prey in the water.

The venom of the fishing spiders paralyses the prey very quickly, allowing it no chance to escape by diving down into the water. Prey is always taken to the bank or to some floating object before being eaten.

MARINE SPIDERS

No spider lives in the open sea, but several species have managed to carve niches for themselves on the seashore. *Desis marina* from Australia and New Zealand is one of the most successful. About 8mm (0.3 inch) long and coloured rust and cream, it lives on coral reefs and intertidal rocks and feeds on sandhoppers at low tide. Like *Dysdera*, it has relatively huge fangs for dealing with these crustaceans. The spider's home is the vacated burrow of a worm or some other creature, to which it returns as the tide comes in. A lid of closely woven silk keeps the water out and protects the spider until the tide goes out again.

THE AMBUSHERS

These are the spiders that lie in wait for their prey and grab it when it comes within range. This can be a fairly chancy way of getting food because suitable prey does not arrive on demand, but spiders can usually go without food for weeks or even months and the problem is not quite as great as it might seem. In addition, the spiders can also go off to search for food or to take up another station if they get really hungry. Instinct usually ensures that they take up stations in the right sorts of places to get a reasonable amount of food. Many ambushers hide in burrows or other retreats, often employing silk strands to inform them of the arrival of prey, but others sit freely on the ground or on the vegetation and detect approaching prey by sight or by picking up vibrations.

Crafty crab spiders

The crab spiders of the family Thomisidae are the best-known exponents of the ambush. There are about 3,000 species, mostly with squat, crab-like bodies and all with the front two pairs of legs much longer than the rest. Very few species are more than about 20mm (0.8 inch) long. The spiders don't move a lot, but when they do go walk-about they move with a distinctly crab-like sideways or diagonal gait. Many crab spiders are beautifully coloured, although never as gaudy as the jumping spiders, and they often carry an assortment of 'warts' and other tubercles – especially the females. With a few exceptions, such as *Heriaeus hirtus*, they have no prominent hair. Males are frequently less than half the size of the females, although they have relatively long legs, and their colours are often quite different.

Many crab spiders lurk in flowers, which are obviously good places for catching insects, but others prefer foliage or tree trunks and some loiter on the ground or in turf. Although many have bright colours and markings, they usually sit so still and blend so well with their surroundings that they are not at all easy to spot. *Diaea dorsata*, for example, is a tree-living British species with bright green legs and front end and a brown rear and is very hard to detect on a background of twigs and foliage, while the hairy *Heriaeus hirtus* of Continental Europe blends beautifully with bristly grass heads. Camouflage of this kind is concerned primarily with protection but, as we shall see, some crab spiders also employ camouflage to deceive their prey.

Keeping a firm footing with their rear legs, the spiders extend their front legs and wait for dinner. The crab spiders' eyes, arranged in two rows, are not as good as those of the wolf spiders and jumping spiders. The two outer

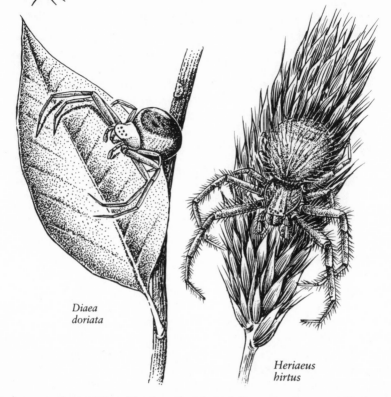

*Diaea
doriata*

*Heriaeus
hirtus*

The brown and green Diaea *blends well with the foliage of various trees.* Heriaeus *is
abnormally hairy for a crab spider and lurks almost unseen on hairy grass spikes.*

eyes in the bottom row are usually much larger than the rest and can focus
clearly only on objects within a few millimetres. The other eyes can pick up
movements as much as 20cm away, but the spiders rely mainly on
vibrations to tell them that food is on its way. This means that they can feed
by day and by night, although the usual prey of the flower-inhabiting crab
spiders are day-flying insects.

With a potential victim in the offing, the spider shuffles smoothly round
to face the incoming vibrations, and as soon as the victim comes within
range of the spiny front legs it is grabbed. Because it has no web to restrain
its victims, the crab spider needs a quick, clean kill and usually goes for the
jugular, sinking its fangs deep into the victim's neck where the major nerves
are situated. If the first bite is not in the right place the spider will usually
turn the prey round until it finds the correct target. The fangs are quite
small, but the venom they inject acts very quickly against insects and other

NEARLY IN THE SOUP

Misumenops is a small crab spider that lives dangerously. It takes up residence in the traps of various pitcher plants living in south-east Asia. Flies are attracted to the pitchers by colour and scent and in the normal course of events they fall into the pitchers to be digested and to augment the plants' nitrogen supplies. But *Misumenops* diverts some of the flies into its own energy system. A special protective coating ensures that the spiders themselves are not digested if they slither into the slurry of decomposing insects at the bottom of the pitchers.

arthropods. Crab spiders are thus able to tackle bees, butterflies and other insects much larger than themselves. The prey is never wrapped in silk. Flower-frequenting species do not usually bother with small prey and completely ignore the small beetles crawling in the same flowers, but ground-living crab spiders specialize in crawling insects and usually recoil from flying insects. Although their venom is deadly to their normal prey, the crab spiders are all completely harmless to people.

A crab spider's fangs have no teeth and the spider does not macerate its prey. The fangs simply inject juices that digest the soft tissues, and then the spider sucks out the resulting solution, leaving an empty, but otherwise perfect specimen, for which many entomologists have been very grateful.

Masters of camouflage
Many flower-inhabiting crab spiders are able to change their colours to some extent to match different flowers. *Misumena vatia*, which occurs all over the Northern Hemisphere, varies from white to deep yellow, and the abundance of white and yellow flowers in spring and early summer means that it is never short of suitable flowers. Spiders put on the 'wrong' flowers often crawl away and search for more suitable ones, but if they are prevented from moving they will change colour in a day or two to blend in with the new background. The rather angular *Thomisus onustus*, which lives in many parts of Europe, including Britain, exists in white, pink and yellow forms, but has only a very limited ability to change colour – between white and pink and between white and yellow. Each individual selects a flower of the appropriate colour and usually stays there until the flower fades.

These spiders undoubtedly gain some protection from birds by blending in with the flowers, but experimental work involving putting coloured beads and pebbles on dandelions and other yellow flowers has shown that

The crab spider, Thomisus onustus, *about 7mm long, sits in flowers in such a way that it can plunge its fangs straight into the necks of visiting bees and other insects.*

such concealment is also jolly handy for getting grub. In one such experiment, ten times more bees and hover-flies visited flowers carrying yellow pebbles than visited flowers with black pebbles.

Phrynarachne decipiens from south-east Asia doesn't hide from its victims: it lures them right into its embrace. The black and white spider spins a small pad of silk on a leaf and then sits on it, giving a very good

impression of a bird dropping that has fallen on to the leaf. Flies and even butterflies frequently visit bird droppings, from which they get valuable minerals, but if they mistake the spider for one they are quickly snapped up. As well as deceiving its prey with this scheme, *Phrynarachne* must get a good deal of protection from birds, which presumably take little notice of their own excrement.

Crab spider look-alikes

Spiders of the family Philodromidae are superficially similar to the crab spiders, and were at one time included with them in the Thomisidae, but their legs are all more or less the same length and the carapace is distinctly

---

DANGEROUS PERFUME

The orchard spiders (*Celaenia* species) of Australia and New Zealand are orb-web spiders that have given up making webs. They spend the daytime sitting absolutely motionless on the leaves of various trees and shrubs, and, with their legs folded tightly against their rather lumpy and irregular bodies, they are usually mistaken for bird droppings. They are often called bird-dropping spiders. Many nights seem to be spent in exactly the same position, but occasionally – presumably when they feel hungry – the spiders hang from the underside of the leaf or lower themselves on a short thread and wait with their spiny front legs extended in the manner of crab spiders. For many years it was unknown how these lethargic spiders managed to catch any food, but we now know that *Celaenia* is a treacherous siren. The adult spiders feed entirely on certain noctuid moths, and careful examination of their captures has shown that they always catch males.

The spiders give out scents that resemble the pheromones used by the female moths to attract their mates, so the male moths come flocking – not to the expected embrace of a female, but to death in the arms of the spider. Recent observations suggest that the spider can alter its scent from time to time as it grows up – and thus make use of different kinds of moths. The youngest spiderlings are believed to attract small midges, although it was once thought that they made orb-webs to trap prey until they were large enough to tackle moths.

Snaring or ambushing with the aid of scent is undoubtedly the final stage in the reduction of the orb-web, earlier stages of which are represented by the bolas spiders (see page 71). Although it makes no tangible trap, it could be argued that *Celaenia* is a trapper and not an ambusher, because its scent snares its prey as effectively as any web.

circular. Although these spiders are fairly sedentary creatures, and usually well camouflaged in their natural homes, they don't wait for prey to come within their grasp: they are essentially hunting spiders and they embark on high-speed chases as soon as they detect anything moving within a few inches. Some species, including the dune-dwelling *Philodromus fallax*, hunt on the ground, but many are good climbers and hunt on the vegetation. *P.*

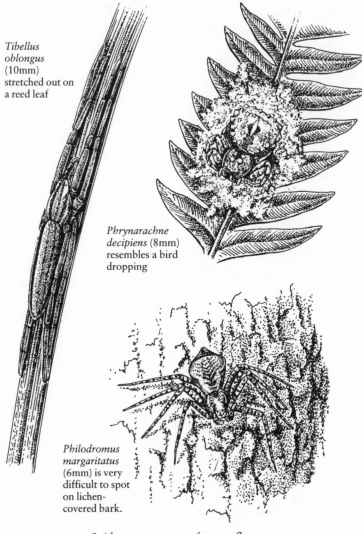

Tibellus oblongus (10mm) stretched out on a reed leaf

Phrynarachne decipiens (8mm) resembles a bird dropping

Philodromus margaritatus (6mm) is very difficult to spot on lichen-covered bark.

Spiders are masters of camouflage.

margaritatus, another British species, lives on tree trunks and its black and grey body looks like a lump of lichen. *Tibellus oblongus*, widely distributed in the Northern Hemisphere, including the British Isles, is a bit of a deviant in that it has a long, slender body, but this is ideally suited to the spider's habitat. It lives in long grass, especially in damp habitats, and is not easy to see when stretched out along a leaf blade. *Tibellus* could be confused with the web-spinning *Tetragnatha* species that live in similar habitats, but *Tetragnatha* does not have a circular carapace.

Trapdoor spiders
The handiwork of a trapdoor spider might not be quite as elegant as that of an orb-web spider, but its burrow is a remarkable bit of animal engineering and has rightly been called a triumph of protective architecture. There are thousands of burrows to the hectare in some places, but they are so well camouflaged that you can walk over them without being aware of them at all. Trapdoor spiders are mygalomorphs belonging to the family Ctenizidae. Most of the 700 or so known species live in the tropics, but several species live in southern Europe and the southern United States and there are also plenty of these fascinating spiders in Australia and New Zealand.

The spiders are up to about 3cm long and solidly built like all mygalomorphs, with some pretty hefty armour at the front end. Their fangs or chelicerae each carry a rake of strong spines used for digging the burrows. The palps and front legs also help by scraping away the loosened soil. Excavated soil is periodically brought out, held in the spider's folded fangs, and dropped a short distance from the burrow mouth. So good is the camouflage of the finished burrows that these little piles of soil are often the only way of finding the spiders.

The burrow is up to 30cm deep, and when digging is complete the spider stabilizes the walls by smearing them with saliva and pounding them with its palps. A silk lining is then added. It is completely closed like a sausage skin at first, but the spider later slices round the top to form the lid or door. About a third of the circumference is left intact to form the hinge. Some trapdoor spiders add a narrow flange or brim and stick a few bits of debris to the upper side of the lid for camouflage, but others make much thicker lids which fit the burrow openings like corks. These lids are made with many layers of silk and soil particles and are cleverly bevelled to provide a tight fit. The lower surface is closely woven and has a felt-like texture. When the spider is at home it often bolts the door by anchoring its legs to the wall of the burrow and sinking its fangs into the lid. A considerable pull is then needed to open the door. The trick is to stamp hard in the vicinity of the burrow: the scared spider drops to the bottom of its burrow and then the lid

can be gently lifted with the blade of a knife. Luckily for the spiders, their enemies don't know this trick, although some spider-hunting wasps have no trouble in chewing through the lids.

Trapdoor spiders are definitely agoraphobic and don't like to leave their homes. Many females spend their whole lives in their burrows. When they are hungry, most trapdoor spiders simply lift their lids a little and lie in wait. Some wait for prey to walk right up to them and then make a quick lunge with their front legs: the hind legs remain anchored in the burrow for a quick retreat. Other species, alerted by vibrations, dart out to catch anything that walks by, but they never go very far and always dive back into their burrows as quickly as possible. Crickets, grasshoppers and beetles figure largely in the prey of these large spiders. Several species fix silken trip-wires to the mouths of their burrows for better early warning, and the large

TREE-TRUNK TRAPDOORS

Spiders of the family Migidae resemble the true trapdoor spiders but they are a bit smaller and they lack the rakes on their chelicerae. Instead of burrowing in the ground, most of them construct their tubular dwellings on rough tree trunks. In New Zealand they are called tree trapdoor spiders. Fragments of bark are woven into the tough silken tubes, which are often so well camouflaged that they are invisible from just a few inches away and can be located accurately only by touch. Some species build on rock faces, especially on coastal cliffs, and conceal their tubes with bits of lichen and general debris. This family occurs mainly in Australasia and South Africa.

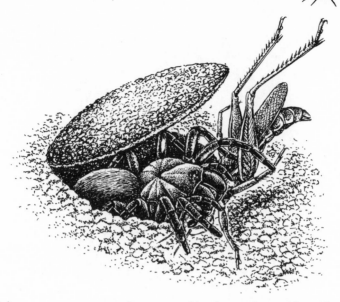

A quick lunge at an unwary grasshopper provides the trapdoor spider with another meal.

Australian *Anidiops villosus* is one of several species that extend their areas of detection by arranging twigs around their burrows and then sitting with their feet resting on the twigs. Most trapdoor spiders open up at night, but some species never open their trapdoors at all until something walks over the top.

The purse-web spiders

The purse-web spiders of the family Atypidae are closely related to the trapdoor spiders but their shelters are sealed tubes up to about 45cm (18 inches) long and about as thick as a finger. The tube is made of densely matted silk and is partly buried in the ground, but the upper part lies on the surface or is draped against the lower part of a tree trunk. The exposed part of the tube is well camouflaged with debris woven into its fabric. The spider spends most of its time resting in the subterranean reaches of its tube, but rushes up whenever an insect walks over the exposed section and stabs it unerringly through the tube wall with its long, parallel fangs. The teeth on the basal parts of the fangs then saw through the wall and the victim is dragged inside. The slits are quickly repaired with more silk and the spider retires to the lower reaches of its den to enjoy its meal.

Although the purse-web spiders detect prey by vibrations of the tubular

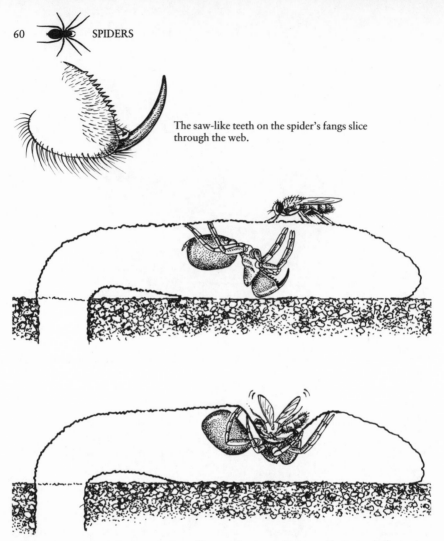

The saw-like teeth on the spider's fangs slice through the web.

The purse-web spider in action, stabbing a fly through the wall of its tubular web with its dagger-like fangs and then dragging it into the tube. The spider is up to 15mm long.

web, the web does not actually trap the prey and we can legitimately treat these spiders as ambushers rather than trappers.

Atypus affinis, Britain's only mygalomorph spider, is sometimes called the British trapdoor spider. It inhabits well-drained slopes, mainly in the southern counties, where the exposed part of its tube can be found among the grass tufts. The spider is widely distributed elsewhere in Europe, but does not occur further north than Denmark.

Deadly funnel-webs down under

Australia has more than its fair share of venomous creatures, including snakes and jellyfishes as well as spiders. The most infamous of the spiders are the various species of *Atrax*, popularly known as funnel-webs although not to be confused with the web-spinning agelenids that are often given the same name. Funnel-web spiders are mygalomorphs and closely related to the trapdoor spiders and, although they make no trapdoors, Australians often refer to them as trapdoor spiders. The Sydney funnel-web (*Atrax robustus*) is the most dangerous of the eight or so species. It used to hit the headlines every now and then when someone died after being bitten, but antivenins are now available and no deaths have been recorded in recent years. The species is quite handsome as spiders go, with a shiny chestnut brown or black carapace, a velvety black rear, and a beard of red hair around its fangs. Females are up to 5cm (2 inches) long. Males are rarely more than half that size, although their legs are longer.

The spiders live in underground burrows up to 30 cm (12 inches) deep. They prefer to use existing holes and crevices, although they are perfectly capable of excavating their own homes with the aid of their fangs, and many of them set up home under stones and fallen logs. Garden rockeries and log-piles are favourite spots, so sturdy gloves are in order for gardening. The burrow is lined with silk, which extends from the mouth to form a funnel. Trip-wires radiating from it warn the spider of approaching prey. Beetles and other large insects are the main prey of the funnel-webs, but they also snap up other spiders. The burrow entrance is often littered with wing cases and other tough bits that the spider cannot deal with.

Females rarely move far from their burrows, but the males roam freely in the summer as they search for mates. Bites from wandering males are more common than bites from females and, although very painful, they are not deadly – the poor old male does not have as much venom as his mate. Bites from females are usually received when the spiders' lairs are disturbed while gardening or gathering logs. When annoyed, the spider raises the front half of its body, with its front legs held high and its fangs exposed and ready to inject their fearful cocktail of pain-producing chemicals. A glistening drop of venom can often be seen at the tip of each fang. With a length of about 5mm (0.2 inch), the fangs are longer than those of many venomous snakes, although they are a fair way down the league table of spider fangs.

THE TRAPPERS

Apart from man and a few insects such as the ant-lions, the spiders are the only animals that set traps to catch their prey. Their delicate webs are beautifully designed to trap the maximum amount of prey – mainly insects – for the minimum outlay in silk and energy.

Silken signatures
The variety of spider webs and snares is almost as great as that of the spiders that make them and, although it is not always possible to name a spider merely by looking at its web, it is often possible to put it in its correct family, or even genus. Near-vertical orb-webs containing a distinct hub of silk threads can be confidently assigned to the family Araneidae, and there is no mistaking the webs of the Amaurobiidae that decorate old walls and tree trunks like little lace doilies (see page 81).

Glistening orbs
The most familiar of all spider webs are the orb-webs of the garden spider and its relatives in the Araneidae. These webs are very close to vertical and they festoon fences and vegetation all over the world. They range from the huge nets of the tropical *Nephila* species, which are as much as six feet in diameter, to the lilliputian webs of the little green *Araniella cucurbitina* which are often stretched across a single apple leaf. Orb-webs, at least in temperate climates, are most often seen in the autumn, leading many people to believe that this is the only time that the spiders are active. But the spiders are functioning for much of the year – certainly all through the summer: their webs are not so obvious then because the spiders are younger and they make smaller webs – and they lack the sparkle added by the dews and frosts of autumn. The spiders sitting in or near their webs in the autumn are usually plump females and this leads to another false assumption – that males do not make webs. Of course they do – how else could they get their daily grub? The fact is that male spiders mature earlier than the females (see page 95) and abandon their webs in search of other worldly pleasures. As most observations and descriptions of spider webs have involved mature females, it has become almost a convention to refer to the spider as 'she', but it should not be forgotten that the males behave in a very similar way until they grow up.

Constructing the orb-web
Over the centuries, the construction of orb-webs has been studied by many people, including the great French naturalist Henri Fabre, who once

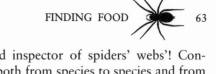

described himself as a 'self-appointed inspector of spiders' webs'! Constructional details vary considerably, both from species to species and from one observer to another, but the following basic plan of campaign is followed by all araneid orb-web builders.

The first essential is to establish the bridge thread, from which much of the finished web will be suspended. There are two ways of getting this bridge thread into position. Generally, the spider pulls a short drag-line from her ampullate glands, anchors it at a convenient spot, and then trails it behind her as she explores the area for another suitable anchorage. She then pulls the line tight and fixes it firmly in place with silk from her pyriform glands. The second method of establishing the bridge thread is a bit of a hit and miss affair. The spider draws out a short drag-line and waits for the wind to catch it. The pull of the wind drags more silk from the spinnerets and the thread eventually clings to a branch or some other support. Using her remarkable ability to assess the tension of the line, the spider tests the safety of her tightrope, and if all seems well she makes the crossing and anchors the far end securely. This is the method by which spiders manage to hang their webs over streams and wide woodland paths, but the final position of the web depends entirely on the direction of the breeze.

The initial bridge thread is very flimsy and the spider quickly strengthens it by scurrying to and fro with more strands of silk. On her first crossing, she may actually eat the old silk as she goes, so that her body forms a living link between the old silk in front of her and the new silk that she trails behind her. With her bridge secure, she can embark on the next stage, which commonly involves spinning a fairly slack thread that hangs from the two ends of the bridge like a washing line. Lowering herself on a new thread from the centre of this line until she reaches a safe perch, the spider hauls on the new thread and pulls the 'washing line' into a V. The base of the V becomes the centre of the web, and the difficult part of the business is then over. By scampering up and down the three primary spokes or radii, with silk constantly flowing from her spinnerets, the spider rapidly forms the rest of the framework and adds the rest of the radii. Adult spiders usually install fewer radii than young ones, but otherwise each species has a fairly constant number of radii in its web. As a rule, bigger spiders make bigger webs, but the shape of the frame is entirely dependent on the available supports.

When the radii are all complete, the spider ensures that they remain in place by laying a loose spiral of silk over them, starting from close to the centre and working her way to the outside. Up to this point, the silk has all been drag-line stuff from the ampullate glands, but the final stage of construction calls for some sticky stuff. Starting from the outside, and eating

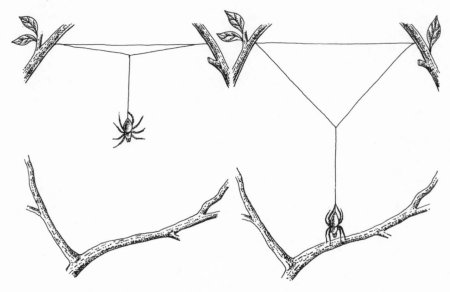

Dropping from the centre of her slack line . . .

. . . the spider pulls the line taut to make the first three radii.

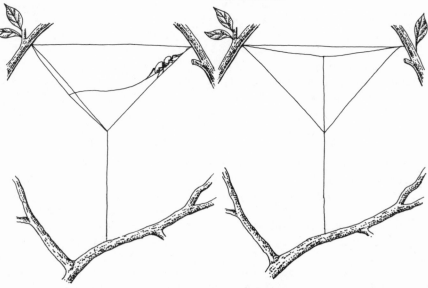

Trailing silk as she scampers along the initial radii . . .

. . . she begins to add more spokes to the upper part of the web.

The building of an orb-web.

Frame threads are fixed to suitable points and the radii are completed.

The loose, dry spiral is laid to hold the spokes in place and then . . .

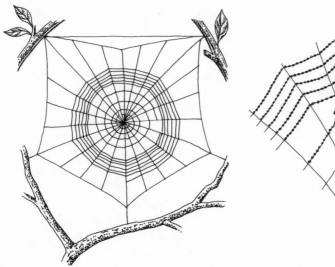

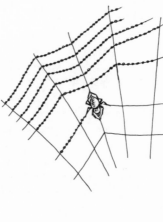

. . . working from the outside, the spider lays the sticky spiral.

As the spider stretches the silk, the gum breaks into droplets strung out along the threads.

the loose spiral as she goes, the spider begins to lay down the catching spiral, using silk from her flagelliform glands. The silk is coated with gum from the aggregate glands as it leaves the spinnerets, but as the silk is stretched the gum breaks into tiny droplets strung out along the thread – droplets that are responsible for transforming the webs into shimmering filigree when touched by the morning dew. Although the silk of the catching spiral is more or less continuous, it does not form a true spiral. The hub of the web is usually a bit above the centre and there are significantly more arcs of silk below it than above it – laid down as the spider moves to and fro under the hub like the bob of a pendulum. Using her legs as rulers, she fixes the silk in place with amazing speed and accuracy, although she has never had a geometry lesson in her life! The whole process is usually completed in less than an hour – often much less – and everything is done by touch: covering their eyes does not impair the spiders' web-making abilities in any way.

The catching spiral always stops short of the centre of the web, where the araneid spider spins irregular strands of silk to form a circular disc on which it can rest. The gap between this central disc or hub and the catching spiral enables the spider to nip smartly from one side of the web to the other. The webs of related families, such as the Metidae and Tetragnathidae, can be recognized because they have no central disc. In fact, the tetragnathids remove all the silk from the central region to leave a completely open hub. These webs also lean more than those of the araneid spiders and are sometimes horizontal.

The catch

When the web is complete, the spider settles down to wait for results. Some species rest in the centre of their webs, while others prefer to hide under neighbouring leaves or in convenient crevices – but always maintaining contact with their webs by way of silk threads. As soon as an insect blunders into its web, the spider dashes to the hub and then, guided by the vibrations, streaks unerringly along the right spokes to reach its victim. Specialized claws and bristles on its feet grip the silk firmly (see page 19), and oily secretions stop the spider from getting stuck, although it normally runs only on the non-sticky spokes and usually travels on the lower surface of the web with its body held away from the sticky spiral. If you want to see the spider in action, try tickling its web with a grass stem. A vibrating tuning fork works even better – E above middle C gives a pretty good imitation of the vibrations of a struggling fly and often brings the spider hurrying to invest-igate. The prey is dealt with in a variety of ways. The big *Nephila* spiders of the tropics, for example, normally paralyse their prey with a bite first and then wrap it in silk, but the garden spider and most other orb-web spiders

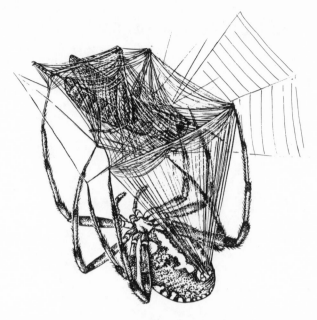

An orb-web spider rapidly draws silk from her spinnerets to parcel up a grasshopper.

do things the other way round – although moths tend to be bitten first because their flapping wings interfere with the wrapping process. Small flies are normally bitten and eaten without being wrapped. The wrapping silk, from the aciniform glands, is drawn from the spinnerets in a broad band and wound tightly around the victim as the latter is rotated by the spider's front legs. Even a large grasshopper can be completely mummified in a few seconds. The meal is then carried to the hub to be eaten – wrapping and all – or else left hanging in the web until required. But there are plenty of thieves about (see page 103) and the spider cannot be sure that the larder will still be full the next day.

Orb-webs are designed to catch insects up to about the size of the spiders themselves. Larger insects are cut out by the spider before they can do too much damage, or else they escape very quickly of their own accord. Moths escape easily, leaving only their detachable scales clinging to the sticky parts of the webs. An orb-web must be able to hold a victim for at least five seconds to give the spider time to reach the hub, determine the position of the victim, and bite or wrap it. The near-vertical webs of the araneid spiders are particularly good in this respect because prey cannot fall straight out – it drops on to the next strand of the spiral. The orb-webs of *Uloborus* species

DECORATED WEBS

A number of orb-web spiders, notably the colourful *Argiope* species, decorate their webs with zig-zag bands of white silk known as stabilimenta. The bands usually form either a cross or a vertical stripe through the centre of the web, although they are not always fully developed. In one study of *A. bruennichi* it was found that about a third of the webs had no

Argiope bruennichi *with her fully developed stabilimentum.*

signs of stabilimenta at all and another third had nothing above the hub. In my French grassland colony (see page 12), the proportion of webs with stabilimenta was less than 1 per cent in September, although webs built higher up in brambles and nettles nearly always had stabilimenta. It was originally thought that the stabilimenta were strengthening devices, but there is no real evidence supporting this idea. The fact that stabilimenta are made only by those spiders that habitually rest in the middle of their webs suggested that they might also serve to conceal or disguise the spiders. This may well be true for those species whose stabilimenta form central discs, and these discs may also act as parasols for the resting spiders: some tropical spiders certainly move to the shaded side of the disc when they get too hot. But it is now generally believed that linear and cross-shaped stabilimenta actually advertise the presence of the webs and prevent birds from flying into them and wrecking them. Another possibility is that the stabilimenta are used as moulting platforms (see page 95). This would certainly explain the common observation that young spiders are more likely to make stabilimenta than mature ones.

are usually horizontal, but they contain hackle-band silk from the cribellum (see page 88) and victims cannot pull themselves free so easily – which is just as well because these spiders have no venom to slow them down.

Web repairs

Despite the elasticity and strength of spider silk, orb-webs are easily damaged by large insects and by strong winds and heavy rain, and they have to be restored quite frequently. A spider will occasionally repair its web if the damage is slight, but complete re-building within the original framework is the normal practice, with the old silk being eaten and rapidly recycled (see page 29). Re-building may start immediately, especially if the spider is hungry, but most spiders have particular times for re-building. The larger spiders tend to restore their webs at night, when they are safe from hungry birds, but early morning is a favourite time for many species and this is a good time to watch them at work. Weather conditions also play a part, just as they do with human builders, and few spiders will attempt any construction work in high winds or heavy rain. Even if the webs are not damaged, they have to be replaced every day or two because the gum becomes coated with dust and loses its stick. Light rain does not damage the web, although it may dilute the glue and cause temporary lack of stickiness.

Economizing on silk

The orb-web is an almost perfect trap for flying insects, providing a good return for the expenditure on silk and energy. But, although the silk is recycled, web production is still a drain on the animal's energy and resources and some spiders have found ingenious ways of cutting down on silk without reducing the efficiency of their snares. *Miagrammopes* species are tropical cribellate spiders, some of which have taken web-reduction to the limit by producing just a single thread. This is a yard or more in length and the spider sprays the central section with a fluffy pad of calamistrated silk which is believed to attract insects looking for a perch. The spider rests at one end of the thread, which she keeps under tension. As soon as a victim lands on the silk, the spider releases the tension and the victim is hopelessly trapped. Some species of *Miagrammopes* spin branching threads, often in several planes, that greatly increase the changes of catching prey. Even with their imitation perches, the threads probably do not catch as many insects as an orb-web of similar dimensions, but considerably less effort goes into making them and it may be that the catch, in terms of numbers per unit length of catching silk, is actually better than that of an orb-web.

Fishing for moths – the bolas spiders

Bolas spiders, also called angling or fishing spiders, live in North and South America, Africa and Australasia. Odd-looking creatures whose squat bodies are often studded with horns and 'warts', they are among the very few araneid spiders whose bites are potentially dangerous to people. Typified by Australia's *Dichrostichus magnificus*, commonly known as the magnificent spider, they cling motionless to leaves and twigs by day and

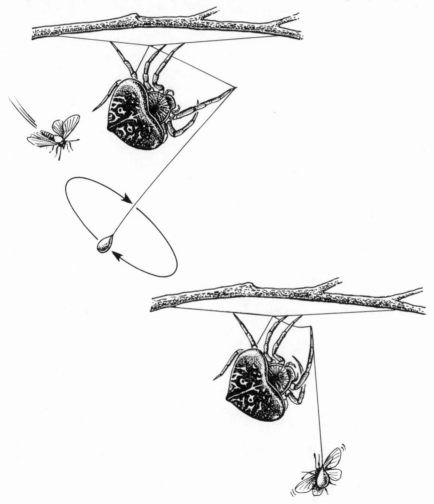

The bolas spider in action, capturing a moth on its single baited line. The glue is very sticky and smells strongly of female moths.

don't stir until nightfall. But they don't go far and they produce even less silk than *Miagrammopes*. Hanging from a short thread attached to the underside of a twig, each spider pulls out a 'fishing line' about 5cm (2 inches) long and carrying one or more blobs of very sticky glue. This is all the bolas spider needs to get a meal. Whirling the line around with one of its legs, the spider waits for a moth to take the bait. This seems a bit of a hit and miss method, and pretty tiring as well, but the spider has a secret weapon in its armoury – a scent just like that released by certain female moths. The male moths can't resist it and come flocking to the spider's line, just as they come to the orchard spider described on page 55. The bolas spider does not usually need to whirl its line around for more than a few minutes each evening.

It is possible that synthetic attractants based on those of the bolas spiders could be used to control certain insect pests. This would be a logical development of the current use of web-spinning spiders to control insects in Israeli orchards and Chinese rice fields.

Triangular webs

Cribellate spiders of the genus *Hyptiotes*, which occur in Europe and North America, build triangular webs, each resembling a section of a typical orb-web. Sitting at the apex of the triangle, with its hind legs firmly anchored to a silken pad, the spider actually forms part of the trap mechanism. It pulls the web taut with its front legs, coils the slack against its body, and waits. When an insect flies into the web the tension is released and the victim is immediately enveloped by the flocculent hackle-bands.

Triangular webs are also made by several tropical araneid spiders, including a species of *Pasilobus* from New Guinea. These webs are horizontal, and that of *Pasilobus*, first described by Michael and Barbara Robinson, contains just three diverging frame threads. The spaces between these three threads are each crossed by several sticky threads that hang in glistening loops. The cross threads are only loosely attached to the outer edges of the web, and as soon as an insect bumps into one of them the attachment gives way, leaving the sticky thread hanging from the central strand, with the victim firmly glued to it. The spider immediately zips along the central thread and hauls up its meal. The web is about 50cm long and its hanging loops give it a surprisingly large catching zone. Moths are almost the only prey of this araneid spider.

Gladiator spiders

Also known as ogre-faced spiders because of their huge eyes (see page 17), the gladiator spiders inhabit most of the world's tropical regions as well as

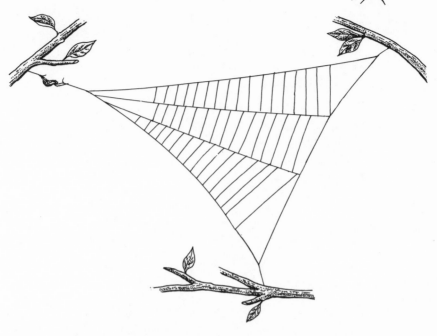

The triangular web of Hyptiotes, *with the spider ready to spring it as soon as an insect arrives.*

some of the cooler parts of Australia and North America. They live in dense scrub, sitting motionless in the daytime when their slender bodies are easily mistaken for twigs. Waking at nightfall, each one selects a spot with a bit of room beneath it and, while hanging from a flimsy scaffold, constructs a highly elastic net with calamistrated silk. The net, which is no bigger than a standard postage stamp, is held by the back legs at first, but when it is complete the spider turns round and grabs a corner with each of its front four feet. The spider then hangs head down and waits. Its eyes, with their amazing ability to gather and concentrate light, can spot movement on the darkest night, and when anything comes within range the spider stretches its net and thrusts it forward over the luckless victim. Even if it has not been used, the net is usually rolled up and eaten at daybreak and the spider goes back to sleep. A new net is made each evening.

Shimmering hammocks
Meadows and pastures often turn into shimmering silver carpets on autumn mornings, when the dew touches the sheets of gossamer that clothe almost

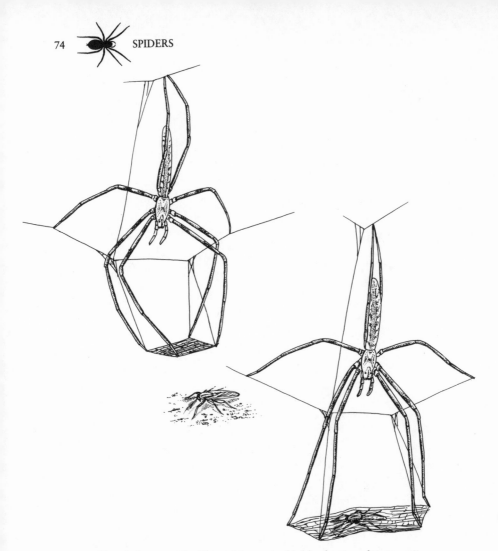

The gladiator spider (Dinopis) *puts its highly elastic web into action.*

every square inch of the grassland. These silk sheets are the handiwork of
the little dark spiders that are commonly called money spiders. When laden
with dew, they sag like hammocks, but at other times they lie flat or even
bulge slightly upwards. Larger, but otherwise similar sheets or hammocks
can be seen on almost every bush and hedgerow branch in the autumn.
Some of them are as big as dinner plates. The makers of all these hammocks
belong to the family Linyphiidae, which is particularly characteristic of the
cooler regions. About 40 per cent of British spiders – over 250 of the 620 or
so known species – belong to this family, compared with only about one per

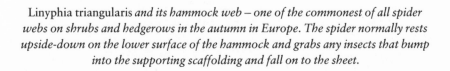

Linyphia triangularis *and its hammock web – one of the commonest of all spider webs on shrubs and hedgerows in the autumn in Europe. The spider normally rests upside-down on the lower surface of the hammock and grabs any insects that bump into the supporting scaffolding and fall on to the sheet.*

cent of Brazilian spiders. *Linyphia triangularis*, abundant on shrubs and hedges all over Europe, can be recognized by its distinctly triangular abdomen with a row of dark, triangular marks along the centre. All of 6mm (0.25 inch) in length, it is one of the largest members of the family and its hammocks are up to 30cm (12 inches) across.

A close look at a hammock web will reveal that the sheet is supported by a maze of 'scaffolding' above and below. The little grassland webs do not have much superstructure, but those built in bushes often have so much rigging above them that they resemble little yachts. The spider has no obvious shelter and spends most of its time resting upside down on the lower surface of the sheet. As well as supporting the sheet, the scaffolding intercepts the leafhoppers, psyllids and other small insects on which the spider feeds. The insects fall on to the sheet and, although the silk is not sticky, they stagger around as their feet get tangled in the loosely woven layers and the spider has no trouble in grabbing them from below and dragging them through the sheet. The web is easily repaired by laying a patch of new silk over the damaged area.

Black widows and other scaffold-web spiders
Scaffold-webs are the domain of members of the family Theridiidae, which are often known as comb-footed spiders because their rear feet are endowed with comb-like rows of bristles – although these cannot be seen without a strong lens because the spiders are all quite small. Theridiids are globular creatures in which the tiny front half is dwarfed by the spherical or triangular abdomen. The web is typically a three-dimensional trellis and is often called a cob-web, although I prefer to restrict the latter name to the scruffy webs and wispy strands of silk found in the neglected corners of buildings. Some of the threads are coated with gum from the aggregate glands, but the arrangement of the dry and sticky threads varies a great deal according to the preferred prey of the species.

The Theridiidae is a large family with over 1,500 species, the best known of which are undoubtedly the black widows – *Latrodectus mactans* and its relatives. These injurious spiders, all with conspicuous red markings on a black body, are found throughout the warmer parts of the world, including southern Europe, and have received an assortment of common names: malmignatte in France, redback or jockey spider in Australia and katipo in New Zealand. The American name of black widow derives from the belief that the female eats the much smaller male after mating; she does sometimes, but probably no more often than many other female spiders (see page 89). The spiders are not aggressive but, because of their potent venom and their liking for human habitation, people do get bitten from time to

The female black widow exhibits the typical globular abdomen of the scaffold web spiders. She is up to 15mm long but her mate is very much smaller.

time. Relatively few bites turn out to be fatal, even without treatment, although there have been many deaths in the last century or so. Of 65 recorded deaths from spider bites in the United States during the 1950s, 63 were due to black widows – the other two were caused by *Loxosceles* (see page 32). Antivenins are now readily available in most areas, although the spiders still pose problems in out-of-the-way places. Muscle relaxants are also valuable in treating black widow victims.

Some biologists consider all the world's black widows to be races of *Latrodectes mactans*, but others believe them to be different species. They certainly have slightly different habits in various areas. The spider is 'urbanized' to a great extent in the United States, and one of the commonest places to find it is around the loo, especially if it is an outside one. A report in the *Journal of the American Medical Association* states that 90 per cent of black widow bites recorded in Texas were received when men were using outdoor toilets! The report gives no dates, and does not say how many ladies were bitten. Dustbins attract nearly as many flies as loos and are equally popular places with the widows. The spiders are also common in and around houses in Australia and New Zealand, where they tend to feed mainly on beetles, but the European malmignatte is much more of an outdoor type, with a liking for olive groves and and wheat fields and the

REDUCING THE SCAFFOLD

Just like the orb-web spiders, several scaffold-web builders have found a way of economizing on silk. *Episinus* species live among grass and other low-growing vegetation and their webs consist simply of two more or less parallel threads running from the vegetation to the ground and linked by a third thread near the top to form an H. The spider hangs upside-down from the cross thread, with its front legs holding the vertical threads near the bottom. Blobs of gum on the lower ends of the vertical threads trap ants and other crawling insects and the spider simply hauls them in and wraps them up.

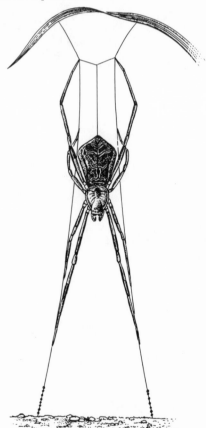

The much reduced web of Episinus angulatus. *The spider is about 4mm long.*

stone walls that surround them. Bites were particularly common at harvest-time (see page 32), and this is when the tarantella musicians reaped most of their rewards as well. Discarded tins and boxes are favourite hiding places for all races of black widows, so tidiness can help to reduce the problem.

A quick glance at a theridiid web suggests a tangled jumble of threads, but it is actually less haphazard than it seems. Although the outer strands may run in any direction, the central ones are arranged in a much more orderly fashion to form the three-dimensional trellis. Many of these central threads are coated with droplets of gum and they can trap some surprisingly large insects. As soon as a victim has been caught, the spider approaches carefully and uses its long back legs to throw strands of sticky silk at it. Not until the victim has been securely bound does the spider get near enough to bite it – usually in the leg. Theridiid spiders have no teeth on their fangs and, like the crab spiders, they simply suck out the liquefied contents of their victims and discard the empty shells. A number of species, including *Theridion sisyphium*, which is very common in British gardens, build thimble-shaped retreats in their webs (see page 80) and retire there to eat their meals. The remains of their victims accumulate in the shelters or are even incorporated into their walls by the spiders, so it is easy to see what the spiders have been eating.

Most scaffold webs are built in low vegetation and their gummy threads are designed and arranged to catch any small flying insects that blunder into them, although some of the spiders are quite capable of dealing with wasps and even locusts. Other species specialize in crawling insects, including ants, and their webs are built to a different plan. *Achaearanea riparia*, a widespread but uncommon spider of European heathlands, is typical of this group. Its flimsy web is slung low down in the heather and contains a relatively huge retreat covered with sand grains and heather fragments. The lower edge of the web is connected to the ground by numerous gummy threads, but these are attached only very lightly to the ground and as soon as an ant or other insect bumps into one of them the attachment snaps. The thread's own tension carries the trapped insect up towards the web where the spider is waiting to haul it in.

Steatodea species are mostly brownish spiders with white patterns on the abdomen. Several of them live in and around houses in many parts of the world, often fixing their webs around window-sills. The web frequently has a conspicuous central platform and it is anchored to the wall by sticky guy ropes that trap crawling insects just like those of *Achaearanea*. The spider usually secretes itself in a crevice while waiting for prey to arrive. The cosmopolitan *S. grossa*, whose female is up to 10mm (0.4 inch) long, is said to prey on black widow spiders in North America.

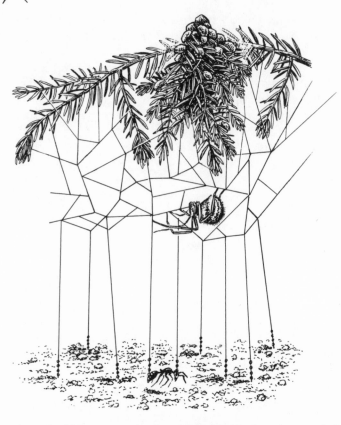

The extensive web of Achaearanea riparia, *with its thimble-shaped retreat, is designed to trap ants and other crawling insects on its glue-studded threads that are lightly fixed to the ground.*

Sheet webs and doilies

Walking over heathland or in rough, grassy places, one cannot help but notice the triangular sheets of silk sprouting from the bases of the plants. These are the work of various members of the Agelenidae, sometimes called grass spiders or funnel-weavers, although they have no connection with Australia's deadly funnel-webs (see page 61). The apex of the sheet leads to the spider's silk-lined tubular retreat, which disappears deep into the vegetation. A careful approach will often reveal the spider peering from the mouth of the tube, but it is a timid beast and a heavy footstep or a careless shadow will send it diving into the darkness. You can try tempting it out again by tickling its web with a grass stem, but do it gently – don't forget you are trying to imitate a struggling fly! These spiders are close relatives of the house spiders that make their triangular webs in the corners of neglected rooms and garden sheds (see page 113). Several other species set up home on sloping ground, with their retreats tucked into crevices between stones.

Old walls and close-boarded fences are frequently clothed with scruffy webs that resemble ragged doilies or lace collars surrounding tubular retreats. These are mostly the work of *Amaurobius similis* and its relatives. The webs are made of calamistrated silk (see page 28) and they trap a wide range of insects crawling on the walls and fences. The insects are usually bitten on the leg and then dragged into the spider's retreat for consumption. New strands of silk are added to the web as required, but there is no obvious pattern. The new silk is usually laid on top of the old stuff and it is this that makes the webs look so scruffy. Try charming the spiders out with a tuning fork – this trick usually works better with *Amaurobius* than with the orb-

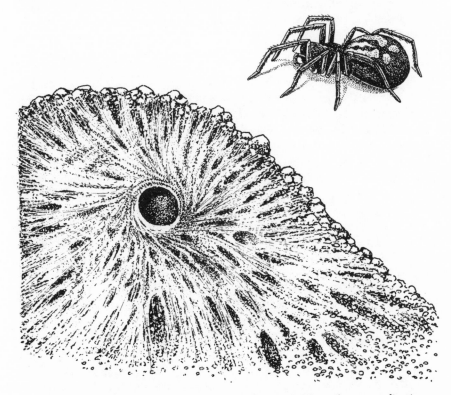

Amaurobius similis, up to 12mm long, with its doily-like web surrounding its tubular retreat.

web spiders. *Amaurobius* species are plump, slow-moving spiders and each one has its preferred habitat. *A. similis*, with a pale brown abdomen marked with darker chevrons, likes fairly dry spots and is very common in the corners of window frames all over Europe. A faint skull-like pattern on its black abdomen gives *A. ferox* a very sinister appearance. Widely distributed in Europe and North America, it prefers damper habitats and is very common in cellars, log-piles, and garden sheds. You can get a pretty clear picture of the spiders' diets by pulling out the webs and examining the debris in the retreats.

Social spiders

Adult spiders are generally solitary creatures, spreading themselves through their habitats so that they share out the available food supplies and also avoid eating each other. Even courting males have to tread very carefully to avoid being eaten by the females (see page 84). But there are about thirty social species, belonging to several different families, that form permanent associations varying from mutual tolerance to true social co-operation. Hunting in groups enables the social spiders to tackle much larger prey than they could if they hunted alone.

The West African sheet-web spider *Agelena consociata* lives in colonies with up to a thousand members, although these colonies are not as tightly knit as some other societies and there is a good deal of interchange between neighbouring colonies. The spiders have been shown to recognize their own species through a pheromone present in the skin. This, possibly combined with a characteristic vibration, prevents them from attacking each other even if they do not originate from the same colony. The members of a colony spin an enormous sheet web on low-growing vegetation and hunt over it in packs, although they don't necessarily all attack at once. A small fly is dealt with by a single spider, but a larger victim will attract several spiders. The larger the victim and the more it struggles, the more spiders pile in to help – a bit like a rugby scrum really! There is, nevertheless, some kind of hierarchy in the colony, with some individuals seemingly a bit above scrummaging for food and preferring to wait for it to be brought to them. The prey is always carried to one of the web's numerous retreats to be eaten, and the meal is shared by as many spiders as can comfortably sit round it. Young spiders always wait for food to be brought to them.

Several other social spiders behave in a similar way, including various species of *Stegodyphus* in Africa and India. Belonging to the family Eresidae, these spiders make huge three-dimensional webs with calamistrated silk. They are so common in parts of India that their webs join up and cover the vegetation for several kilometres.

Several kinds of orb-web spiders, belonging to both the Uloboridae and the Araneidae, live in colonies, although they usually have individual catching webs within their communities. *Philoponella republicana* is a small social uloborid from the forests of Central America. Its colonies, recently described by American spider specialist Yael Lubin, each consist of a vaguely spherical tangle of non-sticky threads up to three metres across, containing a hundred or more spiders, each with its own calamistrated orb-web. These webs, up to about 25cm in diameter, are scattered mainly around the outer edges of the colony and each spider catches its own food, although a certain amount of burglary takes place and individual spiders are sometimes driven from their webs by larger and more aggressive neighbours. Co-operation is limited to the spinning of the main framework of the colony. Courtship and mating usually take place in the central area of the colony, and the females usually hang their egg-sacs there as well. New colonies may be formed when the occasional female moves away from her colony to lay her eggs, but most are formed when groups of hatchlings move away from their home webs and start up on their own. The hatchlings may all be siblings from a single egg-sac, or they may come from several egg-sacs. The weather synchronizes reproduction in the spiders over a wide area, so large numbers of spiderlings are on the move at the same time. Colonies can be found throughout the year, although each one survives for no more than a few months.

Other colonial orb-web spiders behave in much the same way as *Philoponella*, although the arrangement of their catching webs varies a good deal. *Cyrtophora moluccensis* from Papua New Guinea is an araneid, but its catching webs are horizontal and not sticky. They act very much like hammock webs (see page 74) to entangle insects brought down by the surrounding superstructure.

Mixed colonies
Communal webs are sometimes invaded by other spider species. Some of these enterprising lodgers actually erect their own catching webs in the communal framework, but most are quite content to wander over the framework and glean the smaller trifles that are ignored by their landlords. In other words, they act as housekeepers. Similar inquilines can also be found in the webs of various solitary spiders.

Spider sex

A dangerous business
Male spiders are generally a good deal smaller than the females and a courting male has to be very careful. A female can quite easily mistake him for a meal! The male must give exactly the right signals to tell the female who he is and what he wants. His courtship behaviour must also stimulate and arouse the female so that she will co-operate. His courtship signals are often very complex and they involve a variety of sounds and other vibrations as well as visual gestures. Some males placate the females with gifts of food, but others are less gentlemanly and actually tie up the females before getting on with the job.

Alluring scents
Scent was undoubtedly the original method of bringing the sexes together in the animal kingdom, and it is still the primary channel of communication in many animal groups. Most spider groups still use scent for sexual purposes, although they employ other signalling methods as well. Some females, including those of various orb-web spiders, attract males by emitting volatile pheromones into the air, although these do not work over distances of much more than a metre. The majority of scents are associated with the spiders' silk. A male bumping into a female's web detects the scent and then goes into his specific courtship behaviour. And it is not only web-spinning species that lace their silk with scent. Many female wolf spiders smear their drag-lines with pheromones. These scents are species-specific and they are also rather short-lived, so a male neither goes chasing after a female of the wrong species nor does he waste time looking for a female long after she has gone. By giving the male an early warning, the scents enable him to begin his courtship routine in good time and thus reduce his chances of being eaten.

Noisy courtship
Having detected a female, either by scent or by sight, many a male hunting spider sets about seducing her with sound. The females pick up the sounds from the air or from the ground or vegetation and often respond by waving their legs and moving towards the males. The sounds are made by drumming or by stridulation and each species produces a characteristic rhythm to which the female responds. Drumming is usually carried out by tapping the legs or the palps on the ground, although some wolf spiders tap out a rhythm with their abdomens. When drumming on dry leaves they

produce surprisingly loud sounds.

Stridulation produces sound by rubbing one part of the body against another part to set up audible vibrations. Some male wolf spiders use both drumming and stridulation. They stridulate by rapidly flexing and extending the last palpal joint, which contains a minute file and scraper mechanism. The sound travels mainly through the air, but spines on the palps convey the vibrations to the substrate as well. Stridulation is not confined to hunting spiders: many linyphiids (money spiders) stridulate by rubbing their palps against their fangs, while several other groups do it by rubbing the front of the abdomen against the rear edge of the carapace.

Plucking the heart-strings

The males of web-spinning spiders commonly serenade the females by twanging their webs. Female pheromones on the webs ensure that the males don't start plucking the strings of the wrong species. Among the orb-web spiders, the male normally stays near the edge of the female's web, to which he attaches a short mating thread. By plucking this in the correct way with his legs, he entices the female towards him, and mating takes place when she moves on to the mating thread. But not all orb-web spiders behave in this way. The males of several *Argiope* species go straight to the hub of the female's web and begin touching up the female by direct contact.

Wedding presents

The male of the orb-web spider *Meta segmentata* is almost as big as the female and can often be found lounging in the outer part of her web, which he defends against other males. The male and female take no notice of each other until an insect lands in the web. Both spiders rush towards the insect but the male uses his extra-long front legs to keep the female away while he 'gift-wraps' it with a few strands of silk. He then lets her approach the parcel, and while she tucks into the meal he gets on with the job of impregnating her.

The male European nursery-web spider (*Pisaura mirabilis*) also provides a wedding present for his mate, but his interest must first be kindled by the scent of her drag-line. Aroused in this way, he pounces on the first poor fly to appear and quickly fashions a ball of silk around it. Holding it aloft in his fangs, he searches for the female. A receptive female accepts the gift by embedding her fangs in it, and the male then deftly slips beneath her and gets to work with his palps. If he can't catch a fly, the frustrated male may wrap up a seed or a small pebble and present it to the female – and she accepts it as long as it is well wrapped!

Show a leg

Visual courtship signals are used mainly by the long-sighted hunting spiders, especially the wolf spiders and the colourful jumping spiders, and here again the palps and legs form the main signalling equipment. They are usually conspicuously marked and they are waved around like semaphore flags, often accompanied by palpal drumming. Many wolf spiders of the genus *Pardosa* perform energetic dances as they circle around the females, raising each palp in turn and drumming with the other in a sort of spidery hokey-cokey. The semaphore displays of the jumping spiders are particularly spectacular because the palps are often brightly coloured and the inner surfaces of the legs often have brilliant splashes of iridescent colour as well. The males' front legs are somewhat longer and stouter than those of the females because of their signalling function and the spiders have a repertoire of balletic movements and attitudes as wide as any human ballet dancer.

The males initiate the exchanges when they see a female or pick up her scent, and the females often respond by waving their own legs and palps and moving towards the males. Stimulated by this response, the males speed up their displays, and the females then signal their readiness to mate by reaching out and touching the males.

... DIG THAT CRAZY RHYTHM!

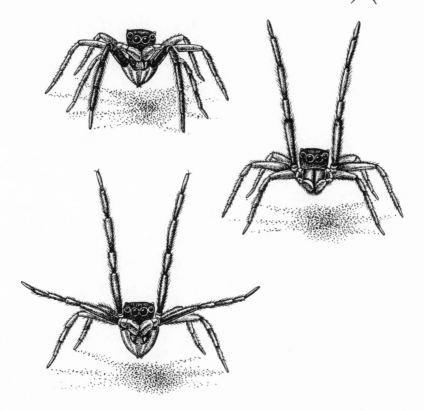

Movements from the balletic courtship dance of a jumping spider.

Unusual genital equipment

A spider's genital organs open on the underside of the body, but the male has none of the copulatory equipment that you might expect to be associated with his genital opening. Impregnation of the female is done by poking her with his enlarged palps, and before he can indulge in any serious philandering he must fill his palps with sperm. He makes a small sperm web, sometimes attached to the female's web, squirts a globule of sperm on to it, and then sucks the sperm into the swollen tip of each palp. Concealed within the tip is an inflatable tubular structure called the embolus that works on the principle of an eye-dropper to suck up the sperm. Among the mygalomorphs and some other groups it is little more than a simple tube, but in most spiders it is exceedingly complex. With both palps charged, the male is ready for action.

The female genitals open near the front of the abdomen or opisthosoma –

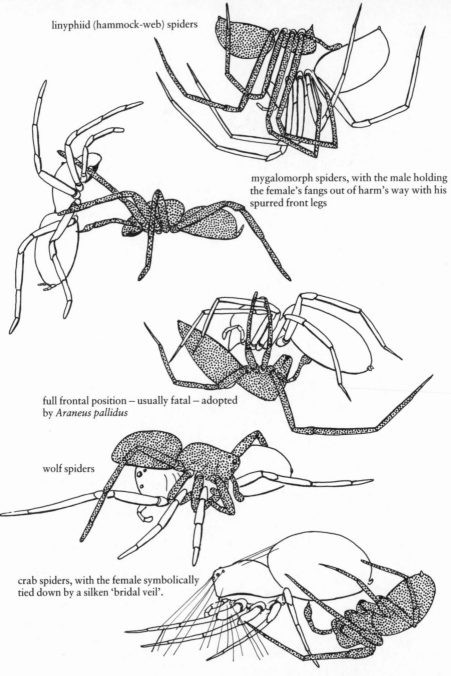

linyphiid (hammock-web) spiders

mygalomorph spiders, with the male holding the female's fangs out of harm's way with his spurred front legs

full frontal position – usually fatal – adopted by *Araneus pallidus*

wolf spiders

crab spiders, with the female symbolically tied down by a silken 'bridal veil'.

Some spidery mating positions, designed to get the male (stippled) past the female's defences and to bring his palps into contact with her genital opening.

the rear half of the body – and a lot of the male's courtship behaviour is designed to get the two spiders into such a position that the male can shove his palps into the correct opening on the female's body. The females of the mygalomorphs and some araneomorphs have only a single genital opening, used both for sex and for laying the eggs, but most female spiders have three openings – two to accommodate the male's palps and one for laying the eggs. In most araneomorphs the openings of the female genitals are concealed by a horny plate called the epigyne. This is often very complex – just like the male embolus, which is the bit that is actually shoved in to the female. The relationship between the epigyne and the embolus is similar to that between a lock and its key and it ensures that the embolus squirts its payload of sperm into exactly the right place. The epigyne also ensures that the male cannot mate with the wrong species, although a male would normally be turned down – or eaten – on the grounds of incompatible behaviour long before he got to put his palps to the test. After mating, many males leave a plug in the female's epigyne, preventing her from mating with other males and thus ensuring the continuation of his own genes.

Mating positions vary a lot. Mygalomorphs usually meet head on and then, holding the female's fangs out of harm's way with the help of a large spine on each of his front legs, the male tilts her upwards and backwards until he can get his palps into her. Among the araneomorphs, some species

DEATH TO THE MALE

It is widely believed that female spiders eat the males after copulation, but this does not really happen very often, even among the infamous black widow spiders (see page 76). Most males escape without problem after mating and then go and do it all over again. The real danger comes before mating, if the female is not ready for it or if she fails to recognize the male's signals. Each male can mate with several females, but the exertion begins to tell after two or three liaisons and reports of males being eaten after mating probably refer to exhausted individuals. Most males give up eating as soon as they mature so, although they are able to store a certain amount of food in their branching food canals, their sexual exploits are performed on a progressively more empty stomach!

There are, however, a few species in which the males regularly end up as food for their mates. The male *Araneus pallidus*, from southern Europe, is one of these ill-fated creatures. The only way in which he seems to be able to get his palps into the female is if she holds him in her fangs – and that's fatal! But at least he contributes towards the nourishment of his offspring.

go for full frontal contact, either head to tail or with both partners facing in the same direction, while others prefer the 'doggy' position with the male caressing the female's abdomen. In species in which the male is a lot smaller than the female he often rides on her back like a jockey, although he may face to the side or to the rear and frequently changes position as he tries to insert his palps.

The male's palps are normally inserted one at a time and each may be inserted several times before the spiders separate and the male goes off to re-charge his palps and search for another female. Although female garden spiders (*Araneus diadematus*) and most other orb-web spiders have usually had enough after about twenty seconds and send their males packing after just one quick thrust, mating lasts for several hours in some species – far longer than is necessary simply to empty the male's palps. Robert Suter and Valerie Parkhill, working with the American linyphiid (money spider) *Frontinella pyramitela* – commonly known as the bowl and doily spider from the shape of its web – have recently shown that spiders mating for longer than the minimum required for sperm transfer may produce larger offspring. It is possible that long copulation allows transfer of other materials that increase the size of the offspring – a useful attribute because larger size means larger webs and more prey, and thus a better survival rate.

BONDAGE AND RAPE

Male crab spiders are not great lovers and, in common with most of the mygalomorphs or bird-eating spiders, they indulge in little foreplay before getting down to the serious business of copulation. The two sexes are brought together by scent, and in most species they merely have to make contact to initiate the love-making process. The male crawls unmolested on to the female's abdomen and gropes for her genital opening with his palps. But some crab spiders do have a little more finesse. There may be a bit of visual and tactile foreplay with the legs and palps, and then the female allows the male to tie her down with a few flimsy strands of silk. She is in no way restrained by this symbolic 'bridal veil', but by this time she is sufficiently subdued to allow the male to have his way with her.

Drassodes lapidosus (see page 40) and some of its relatives go in for rape. A mature male sniffs out the retreat of an immature female and settles down beside it. As soon as the female completes her final moult he moves in and rapes her, while her new coat is still soft and she is immobile and unable to defend her virtue.

The young spider

PARENTAL CARE

The egg sac

Although mygalomorph spiders may wait several months before laying their eggs, the female spider usually starts laying her eggs a week or two after mating. But first she must make the silken sac or cocoon in which all spiders wrap their eggs. The sac consists largely of strongly crimped silk, with a spongy texture and a lot of air trapped between its abundant loops. The silk does not have the strength and elasticity of other spider silks, but it does not need to be strong. Its main functions are to conceal the eggs from their numerous enemies and to insulate them and ensure that the humidity inside the sac remains just right for their development. The spitting spider (see page 41) and the daddy-long-legs spider (see page 114) wrap their eggs in no more than a few strands of silk and the eggs are clearly visible. This tightfisted use of silk may be connected with the spiders' cave-dwelling ancestry, for caves are naturally quite damp.

The egg-sac is fixed to a suitable surface – a stone, a wall, or a plant stem, or perhaps under loose bark – and the eggs are then laid remarkably quickly. The garden spider, for example, can deposit over a thousand eggs in under ten minutes. Each egg is surrounded by a quick-drying liquid which binds them together in a single mass. A female often produces several egg sacs in quick succession.

Agroeca species fix their egg-sacs to grass stems and then cover them with tiny soil particles for added protection. The camouflage makes them hard to see, although the parasitic ichneumons (see page 103) have no trouble in sniffing them out and filling them with their own eggs. There are also spiders that fix leaves together with silk to form pouches for their egg-sacs, giving them extra protection from parasites and small predators.

For many spiders, egg-sac formation and egg-laying is the end of the road. Many females, including those of most orb-web spiders, die within a few days of laying their eggs. But there are many other species that continue to protect their eggs actively for some time. The sac is often kept in the female's retreat until the eggs hatch. The European *Achaearanea riparia* and some of its relatives in the family Theridiidae (scaffold-web spiders) keep their egg-sacs in thimble-shaped retreats slung in their webs, and they raise or lower the sacs to maintain them at optimum temperatures. If the temperature in the retreat of *A. riparia* rises above 36°C the spider lowers her egg-sac right out of the retreat to prevent over-heating, and she moves it back again only when the retreat has cooled to about 21°C. Some spiders build special cocoon-like nests in which they lay and conceal their eggs. *Agelena labyrinthica*, abundant on British heaths and grassland, surrounds her eggs with a large ball of silk within which she constructs a labyrinth of passages. Although the ball is quite conspicuous, enemies find it very difficult to penetrate. The female remains with her eggs in the labyrinth until she dies, and her body is eaten by her offspring when they emerge from their eggs. Even without a retreat, many female spiders defend their eggs vigorously against ichneumons and other enemies. Crab spiders, for example, remain with their eggs until they die.

Carrying the eggs

Female wolf spiders carry their egg-sacs with them, firmly attached to their spinnerets, and can often be seen basking on garden paths and in other sunny spots in spring and early summer. The inner layers of the sac have a spongy texture, with plenty of air spaces between the silk strands, but the outer layers of silk are tightly packed and leathery, with a smooth surface. The whole sac is like a slightly flattened bead and the female does not give it up lightly. If you do manage to detach it she will hunt around diligently until she finds it again, clasping it to her just as a human mother hugs a child and then re-attaching it to her spinnerets. If she can't find it, instinct compels her

A wolf spider carrying her family of newly hatched spiderlings.

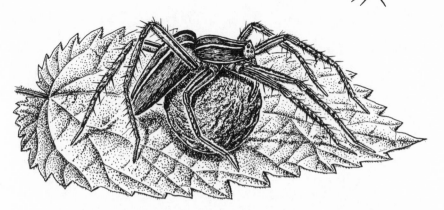

The nursery-web spider (Pisaura mirabilis), *up to 15mm long, has to walk on tip-toe in order to transport the egg-sac attached to her fangs.*

to accept a substitute in the form of a small stone or even an empty snail shell. Almost anything of the right size will be accepted – but only during the first few days. After that, the female becomes so intimately acquainted with her cargo, presumably through its scent, that she will not accept any kind of replacement.

When it is time for the eggs to hatch, the female may use her fangs to slit open the sac and allow the babies to emerge. The babies climb on her back and cling to special hairs there for a few days without feeding, but they gradually drop off and make their own way in the world. Although this is a useful way of dispersing the offspring, they can survive and develop perfectly well without the taxi ride.

The closely related nursery-web spiders (*Pisaura* species) also carry their egg-sacs about with them, but they carry them in their fangs and have to walk on tip-toe in a rather ungainly fashion to accommodate the egg-sac under the prosoma. When the eggs are about to hatch, the female attaches the sac to the vegetation and covers it with the tent-like web that gives the spiders their name. She sits on the web and guards the eggs and hatchlings for a week or so. The hatchlings stay in the web for a few days, moulting once and then gradually dispersing. The raft spiders or fishing spiders (*Dolomedes*) care for their eggs in a similar way, but their tents are much smaller than those of *Pisaura* species.

Feeding the babies

The ultimate in parental care is to feed the babies, but only about thirty spider species take their parental duties that seriously. As we have seen (page 82), some social spiders feed their young, but this behaviour reaches a peak among the comb-footed or scaffold-web spiders of the family Theridiidae. *Achaearanea riparia* and *Theridion sisyphium* both rear their offspring in thimble-shaped retreats, camouflaged with leaf fragments and other debris and slung in the upper parts of their webs (see page 80). The dark brown, globular *A. riparia* lives on heathland and spins its web low down among the heather. A female with youngsters in the nest trusses and bites prey in the web and then summons her youngsters to the dinner table by gently stroking the web.

Theridion sisyphium is another rather small, globular black spider, with white scribbles on her abdomen. She frequents dense bushes and hedgerows. When her babies are very young she feeds them with regurgitated, pre-digested food, but later, like *A. riparia*, she punctures prey and lets the youngsters feed themselves. Swarming up and down the scaffolding like a troupe of trapeze artistes, they soon get the idea and by the time they are a few weeks old and ready to leave home they are well able to deal with small prey on their own. *Coelotes* species live in silken tubes under logs and stones and the youngsters share their mother's home for a while. In the early stages they receive regurgitated food, for which they beg by stroking their mother's legs, but later on their mother begins to share her prey with them. As with many other spider species, the mother dies before the youngsters leave home and they feed on her body before dispersing.

GROWING UP

Most spider eggs hatch within a few days of being laid, although the hatchlings may stay inside their egg-sacs for some time before emerging. The garden spider, for example, lays her eggs in the autumn and the youngsters spend the winter inside the sac before finally venturing out in the spring. Many other orb-web spiders in the temperate regions have similar life cycles, but there are many spiders that lay their eggs in the spring or the summer. In tropical regions breeding goes on all through the year. The spiderlings are usually perfectly formed when they hatch, although they can produce neither silk nor venom until after the first moult. Until then they rely entirely on the yolk stored in their bodies, but this first moult usually occurs quite quickly – often before the spiders leave the egg-sac. Many sacs contain a special chamber in which the youngsters can moult and stretch their tiny legs.

Stripping off

A spider experiences up to fifteen moults during its lifetime, although males, being somewhat smaller, generally undergo fewer moults than females and reach maturity more quickly. Moulting usually ceases when the spiders reach maturity, although some of the long-lived mygalomorphs continue to moult throughout their lives. Periodic moulting, also known as ecdysis, is an essential part of growing up because the spiders, in common with the other arthropods, are encased in a tough outer skin or cuticle that does not grow with the rest of the body. Moulting is under the control of hormones, and when it is about to moult a spider becomes quiescent for a while. During this time the old skin is partially digested and absorbed for recycling, and while this is going on a new, wrinkled skin forms just under the old one. The spider then pumps much of its blood into the front part of its body, where the pressure rises to almost twice its normal value. The old cuticle, now extremely thin, cannot take the strain and it splits along the sides. The top of the carapace comes off like a lid and the splits then continue along the sides of the abdomen. The spider gently heaves its body out of the old skin and then drags its legs out. A lubricating fluid between the old and new cuticles helps the process, but it is still a rather tricky business and the legs often get broken – although they are easily regenerated at the next moult.

The increased blood pressure in the prosoma stretches the new cuticle, which gradually hardens. Much of the blood then returns to the abdomen, leaving room for another period of growth in the prosoma. The abdominal cuticle is a good deal softer than that of the prosoma and it remains fairly stretchable throughout life – which is good news for female spiders whose

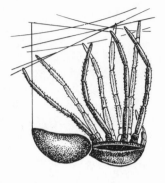

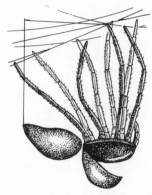

With the spider hanging upside down from its web, the cuticle of the prosoma splits along each side.

The carapace slowly separates from the rest of the prosoma, although it remains attached to the pedicel.

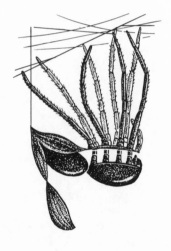

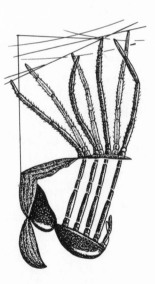

The abdominal cuticle then splits at the sides, freeing the spider's body from the confines of its old coat.

Fangs, palps, and legs are carefully withdrawn from the old cuticle, like fingers being pulled from a glove.

Some stages in the moulting of a web-spinning spider.

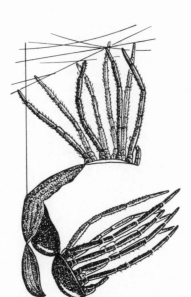

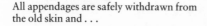

All appendages are safely withdrawn from the old skin and . . .

. . . the spider lowers itself on a thread, flexing its legs from time to time to ensure that the joints remain supple.

bodies fill up with eggs when they are mature. Small spiders can complete a moult in a couple of hours, but larger ones may need several days. Freshly moulted spiders are quite pale for a while and do not regain their true colours for a day or two.

Many orb-web spiders and other web-makers moult while hanging upside down from their webs or from a single thread, but most spiders usually moult in their retreats or in silken chambers constructed for the purpose. Jumping spiders usually build quite elaborate moulting chambers. The old skins can often be found in the retreats.

Up, up and away

Watching a family of young garden spiders swarming out of their egg-sac in the warm spring sunshine, one can get a good idea of just how many eggs may be crammed into a sac no larger than a pea. There may be over a thousand of them, and there is a great deal of competition between the hatchlings. Many of them end up as food for their brothers and sisters, so the sooner they can get away the better. Many of them go in for ballooning. Each little spider draws a short strand of silk from its ampullate glands (see page 25) and then waits for the wind to catch it and pull it out to form a long strand of gossamer. The spiderling is eventually lifted into the air to drift wherever the wind takes it. Charles Darwin recorded numerous small spiders blown into the sails of the *Beagle* when it was over 100 km out into the Pacific, and ballooning spiders have been caught in nets towed by aeroplanes at altitudes of well over 3,000 metres. Clearly, the spiderlings can go far and, although very few of them are likely to land in suitable habitats, they easily can colonize new areas.

All but the largest spider species go in for ballooning, and it is not only the youngsters that take to the air. The little money spiders of the family Linyphiidae are among the commonest members of the aerial plankton.

A young wolf spider about to be carried aloft by the silken 'parachute' being drawn out from its rear end.

How long do they live?
Many tropical and sub-tropical spiders mature rapidly and can produce two or more generations in a year. Most of the spiders living in temperate climates have just one generation in a year and, including the time spent in the egg stage, they live for about twelve months – as long as they can avoid their numerous enemies. Some wolf spiders and jumping spiders may survive for about eighteen months, but the methuselahs of the spider world are the tropical bird-eating spiders or mygalomorphs. Some of these do not even reach maturity until they are about ten years old, and some females have been known to survive for a quarter of a century. This puts them among the longest-lived of all terrestrial invertebrates. Only queen termites are known to live longer – up to 50 years.

Where do they go in the winter?

Flying insects are not common in the winter, so there are not a lot of web-spinning spiders in evidence at this time of year. Most orb-web spiders pass the winter in their egg-sacs – either as eggs or as dormant spiderlings, although the female *Zygiella x-notata* continues to spin her webs around our houses throughout the winter (see page 113). She relies on the hardy winter moths and assorted gnats for food. Hunting spiders commonly hibernate in the soil or leaf litter, usually in an immature state, and, like the eggs, their bodies contain a variety of anti-freeze materials, including glycerol. Some of them build special sleeping chambers with silk and debris. The resting stage is initiated by the shortening of the daylight hours in the autumn and broken by the rising temperatures of spring.

Nevertheless, many spiders do manage to remain active through the winter, thanks to the presence of certain proteins that prevent their tissues and body fluids from freezing. Most of these hardy spiders are wolf spiders and other ground-living hunters and they can survive quite happily under the snow where there are plenty of springtails and small flies for them to eat. They can remain active at temperatures down to −9°C, but the snow cover acts like an insulating blanket and generally keeps temperatures well above this even in very cold spells. The ground temperature under a 20cm layer of snow remains fairly constant at around freezing point, and even 5cm of fresh snow, with plenty of air trapped in it, can prevent the ground temperature from falling much below freezing point.

A few wolf spiders actually hunt on the surface of the snow in mountainous and arctic regions. They find small flies blown to the ground by the wind, but feed mainly on the abundant springtails that exist on wind-blown pollen and other debris (see page 10). But most surprising of all is the existence of little hammock webs in the snow crevices. They belong to various members of the Linyphiidae (money spiders), including *Lepthyphantes cristatus* and *Bolyphantes index*. The latter lives in northern Europe, making its web in the hoof-prints of reindeer and moose and catching springtails there, although the webs are probably used more for mating than for catching food at this time of year – the spiders obviously haven't heard that sex is better in warm weather!

GROWING NEW LEGS

Young spiders are very good at regenerating lost or damaged parts – palps, fangs and spinnerets as well as legs, although it is most often the legs that get broken. If a leg gets caught in any way, the spider can deliberately break it off – very useful if the leg has been grabbed by a bird or a lizard, because it means the spider can scurry away and leave its attacker with just a single leg. The loss of a single leg does not greatly inconvenience the spider, although an orb-web spider might find some difficulty in making a good web without all of its legs. Even two legs can be lost without undue distress. The spider always breaks off its leg at the same point – close to the body between the first and second leg segments – and if the leg is accidentally broken lower down the spider does the job properly and gets rid of the whole limb. The muscles and membranes seal the wound very efficiently, with little loss of blood, and new segments soon start to grow inside the stump. They are revealed at the next moult, perfectly formed, although sometimes a little slimmer and shorter than the original segments. Adult spiders, with no more moults to come, clearly cannot regenerate lost limbs.

The biter bit

SPIDER ENEMIES

Spiders are eaten or otherwise attacked by a huge variety of animals. Starlings are very fond of them, and my garden robin is always ready to pounce on a juicy spider should I disturb one in the log-pile. Bluetits and other insectivorous birds also take spiders when they get the chance, although birds are not as heavily into spiders as many people think – partly because most spiders are active mainly at night. Frogs, toads and shrews eat plenty of spiders, and so do lizards, but it is the invertebrates that are the major enemies of spiders – and other spiders are probably as important as any. Whereas the vertebrate predators take a wide range of prey, the invertebrates are generally specialists and their behaviour is geared up to one particular group of prey animals.

Spider-hunting wasps
Wasps of the widely distributed family Pompilidae all rear their grubs on spiders, which they sniff out with the aid of their antennae. They usually attack spiders as large as or larger than themselves and some right royal

A tarantula hawk, armed with a virulent sting, is a match for even the largest American spider.

battles take place before a winner emerges – and it is usually the wasp. The family includes some of the largest of all wasps, with several American *Pepsis* species exceeding 5cm (2 inches) in length and 10cm (4 inches) in wingspan. These large wasps are commonly called tarantula hawks because they prey on large wolf spiders and even some of the bird-eating spiders. Superior speed and agility enable the wasp to dart in and sting the spider close to its nerve centre under the prosoma, often after dancing around the spider and sometimes throwing it off balance by grabbing one of its legs. The paralysed spider is then dragged away until the wasp finds a suitable place in which to bury it. An egg is laid on the spider and the wasp then seals up the tomb and takes no further interest in it. She goes off to repeat the whole process with another spider. The wasp grub hatching from the egg feeds on the spider which, because it is only paralysed and not killed, does not decay and remains fresh for as long as the wasp grub needs it.

A few pompilids actually enter the spiders' burrows to attack them and thus avoid the chore of digging. The paralysed spiders each receive an egg and are later eaten alive by the wasp grubs. Most of the spiders remain completely paralysed, but some pompilids induce only temporary paralysis and the spiders gradually come round and continue to feed – although much of the food ends up in the wasp grubs riding on their backs. These wasps are thus more like parasites than predators.

Some wasps belonging to the family Sphecidae also rear their grubs on spiders, but these wasps attack small species and put several of them in each nest. These spider hunters often nest in hollow stems, and some build little nests of clay which they stick to stones and other objects.

Ero the pirate

The little globular spiders belonging to the family Mimetidae hunt in the webs of other spiders – usually members of the Theridiidae (scaffold-web spiders) and Linyphiidae (money spiders). They are commonly called pirate spiders, but this is not a particularly good name, because, unlike some spiders described below, they are not interested in robbery: they are full-blown assassins bent on killing the web-owners. Having found an occupied web, the pirate moves stealthily towards the centre and then starts twanging the threads – luring the resident spider to its doom. Some pirate spiders actually lure victims into their clutches by plucking the threads in the manner of courting males. Victims are always caught and bitten in the leg and the venom acts so quickly that they are dead within seconds. There is no need for wrapping! The pirate then works her way from leg to leg and gradually sucks her victim dry. *Ero furcata*, widely distributed over the northern hemisphere, including the British Isles, is one of the commonest of the pirate spiders. A pretty little thing, 3–4mm long with a mottled grey and black abdomen often adorned with brick-red spots, it lives in grassy and shrubby places and attacks spiders of a similar size to itself.

Several other kinds of spiders hunt in the webs of their victims. Most are web-spinners themselves, for they already have the equipment and techniques for moving about in a web, but some jumping spiders also manage to prey on web-spinners (see page 48).

Parasitic insects

Spiders fall prey to many parasitic insects, especially ichneumons, which are related to the bees and wasps. Ichneumons of the widespread genus *Polysphincter* attack orb-web spiders, temporarily paralysing them with a sting before laying a single egg on each one. The ichneumon grub issuing from the egg lives as an ectoparasite, firmly attached to the outside of the spider and gradually consuming its body fluids. The feeding rate of the parasite is such that the spider just manages to hold on to life until the parasite is fully grown.

Several ichneumon genera live as internal parasites, while others attack the spiders' eggs. Using the efficient sense of smell seated in their antennae, the female ichneumons seek out spider egg-sacs and then use their long ovipositors to lay their eggs right inside. When the ichneumon eggs hatch, the grubs set to work to eat the spiders' eggs or the young spiderlings – so these ichneumons are strictly predators rather than parasites. Several groups of flies also parasitize spiders and their eggs. Some ichneumons attack a wide range of host species, but most parasites are more fussy and keep to one host or a group of closely related ones.

The mantis flies – relatives of the lacewings although they bear a remarkable similarity to praying mantises – attack the egg-sacs of many species of hunting spider. The newly hatched larvae search for the sacs on the ground and tunnel into them. They even manage to get into sacs being carried by wolf spiders and nursery-web spiders. Only one larva enters each sac, where it feeds on the eggs and spiderlings until it is fully grown and ready to pupate. Mantis flies are largely tropical and do not occur in Britain, although there are a few species in southern Europe.

Burglars

Numerous spiders have gone in for burglary, otherwise known as kleptoparasitism, and they steal prey from the webs of other species. Most of these burglars are essentially web-spinners themselves, because they already have the know-how for moving about in the webs (see above). Some still make their own webs, but others are obligatory burglars. Some even eat

the silk of other spiders' webs – a good source of protein that is often supplemented by the pollen grains adhering to it.

Several species of *Argyrodes* reside permanently in the big webs of *Nephila* species in tropical America. Some of them take small insects that their hosts would not bother with, but others steal wrapped food and thus inconvenience *Nephila*. If too much of this pilfering goes on *Nephila* may actually move away and set up home somewhere else. Surprisingly enough, the little burglars are rarely attacked. They tend to keep very still for much of the time, moving only when the owner of the web moves and thus avoiding detection.

Even the big bird-eating spiders have to put up with petty pilfering. A tiny spider called *Curimagua bayano* is a highly specialized thief that takes food from the very fangs of bird-eaters in tropical America. Its own fangs cannot open and it has to rely on sucking up fluids from other spiders' victims. It rides to dinner on its host's head, but it is so small that the bird-eaters take no notice of it.

Webs are burgled by several other kinds of animals, notably the scorpion flies. These are real scavengers and eat all sorts of rubbish, including rotten fruit and dead insects. Dead flies are their favourite food and they often raid spiders' webs to feast on the insects trapped there – even pinching flies that the spiders have already wrapped in silk. They sometimes fly off with the loot, but more often settle down to feed in the web. They are in no danger themselves because, if they do get tangled up, they can dissolve the silk threads of the web simply by spitting on them! The same fluid acts as a spider-repellent, so the spiders rarely attack the burglars. A small spider that gets too near may even receive a clout from a scorpion fly's abdomen.

Some tropical damselflies regularly pluck flies from spiders' webs, and also eat the spiders on occasion, but perhaps the most surprising burglars are hummingbirds. They steal the spiders' prey and, like several other birds, they also take a good deal of silk for making their nests.

With so many enemies, it's a little surprising that spiders are quite so numerous – but they do have ways of defending themselves.

SPIDER DEFENCES

The large numbers of offspring produced by many spiders is a reflection of the many dangers that they face during their lives. A large number of babies ensures that at least some will have a chance of reaching maturity – and only two from each pair need to survive in order to maintain a stable population. But large families are not the spiders' only means of coping with the onslaught of their enemies. The forces of natural selection have endowed them with plenty of anatomical and behavioural adaptations enabling them to avoid capture.

Aggression

Many mygalomorphs, including the infamous funnel-web spiders, scare off potential enemies with a show of aggression that usually involves waving the palps and front legs and baring the enormous fangs. The funnel-web may even exude droplets of venom from its fangs, although actual biting is used only as a last resort. Large wolf spiders also go in for threatening displays, which are sometimes made all the more alarming by flashes of bright colour. *Phoneutria fera*, for example, reveals its bright red chelicerae when threatened. We have already seen on page 41 how the spitting spider defends itself, and there are also spiders that fire repellent fluids from the rear end. Some mygalomorphs dislodge barbed hairs from their bodies and throw them at their attackers – often causing great distress to small mammals that get too close, for the hairs can penetrate the skin and cause severe irritation.

Safe houses

Aggressive displays work well for the larger spiders, although most spiders prefer to avoid confrontation altogether and go in for various kinds of concealment and camouflage. Trapdoor spiders might appear to be quite safe in their burrows (see page 57), but they are not entirely secure. Predatory wasps, hunting by scent, have no trouble in finding the burrows and many of the spiders build very elaborate burrows with alternative escape routes or blind side-tunnels which enable them to evade capture.

Cyclocosmia truncata is an American trapdoor spider with an excellent anti-predator device: the rear end of its body is truncated and covered with a tough, circular shield. When disturbed, the spider slips down its tapering burrow until the shield is wedged firmly in place. Not even a large wasp can get past that without digging away the walls of the shaft.

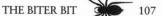

*This trapdoor spider is relatively safe in its
inner chamber, for even if the marauding
wasp manages to open the front door it still has to
get through the second one.*

Camouflage and other tricks

When disturbed, many spiders living above the ground simply pay out a silken life-line and fall out of harm's way. Dangling at the end of the line, they often pull their legs in and are then very difficult to see against the ground or the vegetation. When the danger is judged to be over, the spiders simply crawl back up their life-lines, eating the silk as they go, and continue with their lives. Some spiders, including some tropical species of *Cyrtophora*, drop right to the ground when disturbed and can change colour within seconds to match the darker background. The change is reversible, and normal coloration is usually restored by the time the spider has climbed back up its life-line.

We have already seen that many crab spiders blend beautifully with their surroundings and that some can change colour to match different flowers. Some jumping spiders can also alter their colours to blend in with different backgrounds, but many spiders go much further than this and, through the agency of natural selection, they have come to resemble a variety of inanimate or inedible objects in their surroundings. This form of defence, known as protective resemblance, is best developed in tropical regions, where competition and selective pressures are at their greatest. It is admirably shown by the crab spider *Phrynarachne decipiens* (see page 56) and many others that resemble bird droppings. Many spiders resemble dead leaves, none being better in this respect than species of *Arachnura* from south-east Asia, and other smaller species can be mistaken for buds when resting on twigs and branches. The Brazilian crab spider *Epicadus heterogaster* has several fleshy white lobes on its abdomen and, more than simply blending in with the flowers in which it sits, it really does resemble the petals, thus gaining first-rate protection from its enemies as well as excellent concealment from its prey.

Lobed and decorated abdomens are found in many spiders, including several species of *Argiope*. Often combined with bold patterns, the lobes help to break up the outline of the body and render the spider less conspicuous. Predators that do manage to see through the deception frequently find that the lobes are tough and spiny and not at all appetising.

Camouflage in the web

Many orb-web spiders of the genus *Cyclosa*, including the British *C. conica*, commonly form a vertical stabilimentum through the centre of the web (see page 68) and then coat it with debris, including the remains of their victims. Although such a stabilimentum may make the web conspicuous, the spider itself, sitting in the centre of the web, is very difficult to see. Several other *Cyclosa* species spin circular stabilimenta, and when sitting on these debris-

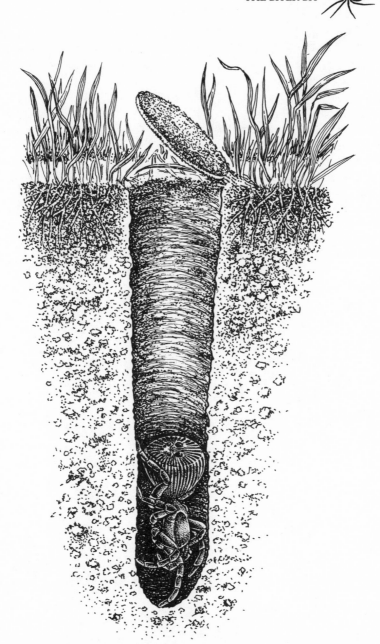

The American trapdoor spider Cyclocosmia truncata *is perfectly protected by its armour-plated backside that fits tightly into the burrow.*

strewn platforms the spiders are even more difficult to detect. And to make themselves even safer, some species construct several circular platforms in their webs to act as decoys and to confuse any predator that might investigate too closely.

Ant mimics

Spiders and other animals employing protective resemblance are attempting – unconsciously, of course – to avoid attention. This form of deception is often called mimicry, but this is incorrect. In true mimicry an animal gains protection by resembling another species that is itself protected by weapons or a foul taste. The most familiar examples are the hover-flies that gain protection from their similarity to wasps. The mimics actually draw attention to themselves by parading their similarities to the harmful models, as if to say, 'Look out, I'm unpleasant.'

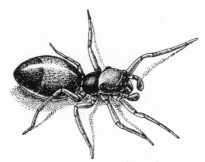

Synemosyna formica (5mm) from N. America

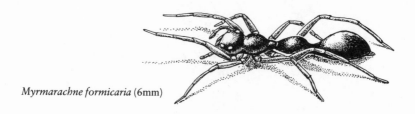

Myrmarachne formicaria (6mm)

Two ant-mimicking spiders.

It is possible that the spider *Argiope bruennichi*, pictured on the front cover, gains some protection from its wasp-like colouring, although it does not behave like a wasp, but the best mimics in the spider world are those that mimic ants. There are hundreds of these mimics, belonging to many different families, and they usually live in close proximity to their ant models. The front of the abdomen is slender, resembling the narrow waist of an ant, but the right behaviour is also important if the spiders are going to fool birds and lizards. The front legs are usually waved about like an ant's antennae – leaving the other six legs for walking in typical insect fashion. *Myrmarachne formicaria*, rare in Britain although widely distributed on the Continent, is one of many similar jumping spiders that mimic ants in many parts of the world. Instead of leaping on to their prey, they lunge at their victims in a manner more in keeping with the neighbouring ants. Most birds and other small predators avoid ants because of their stings and, having learned their lesson, they leave the harmless spiders alone as well.

Spiders in the house

Many spiders, including the fascinating little spitting spider (see page 41), can be found in houses – which, from the spiders' point of view, are not too different from the caves in which many of them once lived. But the most familiar of the household spiders in temperate regions are the long-legged and rather hairy *Tegenaria* species. These are the true house spiders – the ones that scuttle across the lounge floor just as you settle down for an evening in front of the telly. Probably the fastest of all spiders, they can sprint short distances at speeds of about 50cm/sec., so they have often disappeared under the furniture long before you can get up to deal with them. These fleet-footed guests are often males on the look out for females – female spiders, that is! *T. domestica* is a native of the northern hemisphere, but it has followed man all over the world and is now a cosmopolitan

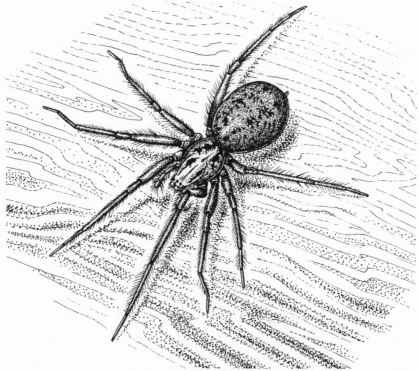

A female house spider, up to 18mm long.

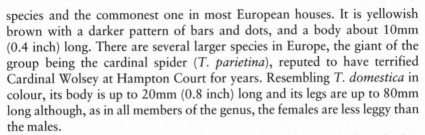

species and the commonest one in most European houses. It is yellowish brown with a darker pattern of bars and dots, and a body about 10mm (0.4 inch) long. There are several larger species in Europe, the giant of the group being the cardinal spider (*T. parietina*), reputed to have terrified Cardinal Wolsey at Hampton Court for years. Resembling *T. domestica* in colour, its body is up to 20mm (0.8 inch) long and its legs are up to 80mm long although, as in all members of the genus, the females are less leggy than the males.

Female house spiders can live for several years, inhabiting sheds and other outbuildings as well as houses. They are especially fond of undisturbed attics and dry cellars, where they drape their familiar cob-webs over everything. The web is a triangular sheet, usually with a tubular retreat at the apex, and a maze of trip-wires all over the upper surface to snare flies and other insect prey. If you can bear to leave the webs in your shed or attic, the spiders will certainly keep down the flies and also the furniture beetles, whose larvae are the dreaded woodworms. In earlier times people had another use for their house spiders – they swallowed them in the belief that this would cure malaria! And in Egypt spiders were regularly put into the beds of newly wed couples in the belief that they would bring good luck.

Another frequent member of the household is the daddy-long-legs spider (*Pholcus phalangioides*). This long-legged and slender-bodied spider usually lives close to the ceiling, where it spins flimsy webs that don't look capable of catching anything, but a fly or another spider stumbling in to one of these webs soon finds itself the target for a barrage of silk threads. Thrown by the spider's long legs, these threads soon entangle the victim and render it helpless. *Pholcus* can deal with prey a good deal larger than itself, but if anything too large enters the web the spider throws itself and its web into a frenzied bout of vibration which eventually throws out the intruder. The female spiders rarely stay in one place for more than two or three days and often play 'musical chairs' as they move around and take over their neighbours' webs. More silk is added as necessary, but the old silk is not re-cycled. In common with most other household spiders, *Pholcus* is more common in older properties than in modern houses, mainly because it does not like the dry atmosphere created by central heating. It is common in southern Europe, including the southern half of Britain, but rare in northern areas. In the warmer parts of the world it is regularly found out of doors.

Several orb-web spiders take up residence around the house, notably *Zygiella x-notata*, whose web is often spun in the corners of window frames and across doorways. The web can always be recognized because two sectors near the top lack spiral threads. The radius running through this otherwise empty space leads to the spider's retreat. The female *Zygiella* is a plump girl, about 6mm long with a dark leaf-like pattern on her abdomen often surrounded by a pink tinge. She is the only orb-weaver spinning webs in the winter in Britain. She can easily be confused with *Nuctenea umbratica*, a very dark, flat spider with a prominently lobed leaf-like pattern on its abdomen. Its natural home is under loose bark, but it now frequents close-boarded fences and sheds. In my house it has taken up residence around the front door, and when disturbed it drops down and dangles menacingly over the threshold – much to the consternation of visitors. Females can be found throughout the year, although they do not spin webs in the winter.

A female daddy-long-legs spider (Pholcus phalangioides) *about 10mm long, clutching her egg-sac firmly in her fangs.*

SPIDERS IN THE BATH

Most people have found spiders in their baths at some time or other. These are usually male house spiders (*Tegenaria* species) that have fallen in while searching for females. Lacking the scopulae (hair tufts on the feet) of hunting spiders (see page 19), they are unable to climb out again and there they must wait until rescued (hopefully) or until some rotter flushes them down the plug-hole. The spiders occasionally fall into baths full of water, and also into sinks and toilets, but as long as the water is not hot, they will not necessarily perish. By closing their book-lungs and tracheae, they can survive in water for half an hour or more, and if you rescue them and put them somewhere to dry they will recover quite well.

Even spiders that appear quite dead can suddenly get up and walk when they dry out and open up their breathing systems again.

Do they come up the plug-hole? In modern houses, where the waste water goes unseen into the drains, the answer is no: and even where the end of the waste pipe is open the chances are slim because the spiders do not like water and will not readily negotiate the water-filled U-bend. But it was a different story in older houses. The bath waste pipe was open at the bottom – often emptying into a funnel on the outside wall – and there was not always a U-bend. House spiders undoubtedly used to make their way into the bath by this route in the past.

Spiders as pets

Spiders are often advertised for sale as pets. These are almost always the larger bird-eaters or mygalomorph spiders, such as the popular Mexican red-kneed bird-eating spider. They are certainly interesting animals, but personally I don't think they make good pets in the normal sense of the word. They are just not active enough, and those that do come out to explore their surroundings tend to be nocturnal. I have played host to several families of daddy-long-legs spiders in my study over the years and been fascinated by their prey-catching abilities, but I prefer hamsters, which will take breakfast with you – or pinch it from your plate when you are not looking!

Nevertheless, many people do like to keep spiders, and with proper attention to their food and humidity requirements the animals can be quite rewarding to the enthusiast. Orb-web spiders are undoubtedly the most interesting, but only when making their webs and wrapping food: for much of the time they sit motionless in their webs or even hide out of sight. Some species can be persuaded to spin their webs in wire loops suspended from the ceiling, but few families will tolerate such decorations in the house and the best place for the spiders is a cool greenhouse with plenty of greenery on which they can build. Other web-spinners, such as hammock-web and scaffold-web spiders, can also be housed in the greenhouse, although there will inevitably be escapes and losses from other causes. Water can be provided by lightly spraying the webs with a mist-sprayer every day or two, and this should maintain a reasonable humidity, although not all spiders actually like damp climates.

Food for the larger spiders can be provided in the form of bluebottles, which are easily reared from maggots bought from a fishing-tackle shop. Even a couple of ounces of maggots will provide far more flies than you are likely to need, but you can adjust the supply by putting the pupae in the fridge – in a closed container, of course, and taking them out as required. The adult flies emerge very quickly after being restored to a warm place. You can throw them into the webs of web-spinning spiders, or just release them into the containers. Smaller spiders are more difficult to feed unless you have access to a supply of fruit flies or other small insects. Greenfly are acceptable to some species, and failing that you could leave a light on in the greenhouse one night a week and leave the door open to allow flies and other insects to enter. Most spiders are happy with one meal per week. In the absence of a greenhouse, you could try keeping web-spinners in large cages made from old net curtains and containing a number of potted plants.

House spiders are easy to keep in an old shoe box, as they don't object to a dry atmosphere and need no water. They can go for a year without food, but appreciate the weekly fly.

Large hunting spiders, including the mygalomorphs, are best kept in an old fish tank or similar container, with a layer of leaf litter and moss and a small glass or plastic container as a shelter. Bluebottles and crickets – the latter often obtainable from pet shops – should keep them happy: even a large spider will not need more than half a dozen flies each week. Smaller hunting spiders, including jumping spiders, can be kept in small plastic containers and fed on springtails sifted from leaf litter, but don't let the containers get too wet inside.

Spiders are not easy to breed in captivity, partly because the female will not always accept the male in the abnormal conditions and also because it is difficult to get enough small prey for the spiderlings, but it is well worth trying.

Harvestmen – the spiders' long-legged cousins

Commonly mistaken for spiders, and often called harvest spiders, these long-legged beasties swarm over rough vegetation and walls in late summer and some species are particularly obvious in the fields at harvest-time. They are called faucheurs (=reapers) in France.

Although they have eight legs and are clearly arachnids, the harvestmen are only distantly related to the spiders. The most obvious difference between the two groups lies in the body. That of a spider has two distinct sections, connected by a narrow waist, but that of the harvestman has no waist: the two sections – the prosoma and the opisthosoma – are broadly connected to form a single, more or less oval unit, although there is often a prominent groove between the two. Body and legs are often rather bristly, and the abdomen or opisthosoma usually carries a dark central mark known as the saddle. British species rarely have bodies more than about 12mm (0.5 inch) and many are very much smaller, although some tropical species reach 20mm (0.8 inch).

Harvestmen usually have very long legs, although some soil-dwelling and litter-dwelling species are short-legged. Ground-dwellers also have tougher cuticles than species living in more open habitats. The second pair of legs are always the longest – a situation rarely found in the spiders – and, together with the palps, they function primarily as sensory organs. Like spiders, the harvestmen can break off their legs when attacked, but they cannot regenerate lost legs.

Harvestmen have just two eyes, which they carry on a turret near the middle of the body. Looking out to the sides of the body, the eyes probably do little more than register light and darkness and perhaps a little movement. Whereas the chelicerae of the spiders form piercing fangs, those of the harvestmen are in the form of minute forceps, used for grasping and tearing food. They have no venom. Harvestmen produce no silk and have no appendages at all on the abdomen. They breathe with tracheae and have no book-lungs. The tracheae open on the leg bases as well as on the sides of the body, and the cephalothorax also carries two repellent glands that open near the front legs. The fluid flowing from these glands has an odour that protects the animals from many potential predators, although not many species can be detected by human noses.

Boffins estimate that there are about 5,000 harvestmen species in the

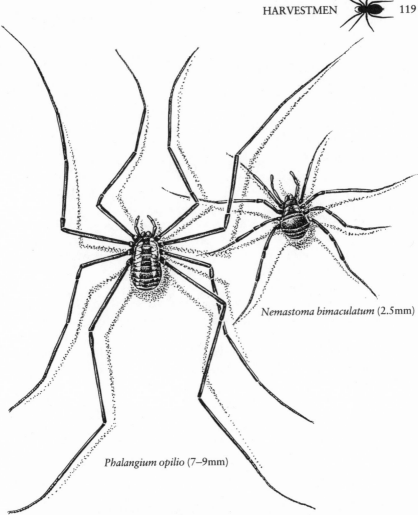

Nemastoma bimaculatum (2.5mm)

Phalangium opilio (7–9mm)

The long-legged Leiobunum rotundum *strides over the vegetation, but the short-legged* Nemastoma bimaculatum *is a ground-living harvestman.*

world, with their headquarters in the tropical forests. They are so abundant in some of these forests that they probably outweigh the spider population. Only about 100 species occur in Europe, and only 24 of these live in the British Isles.

Nocturnal prowlers

Harvestmen are almost entirely nocturnal and most of them hunt in low-growing vegetation, although some of the longer-legged species hunt in

bushes and on walls and tree trunks. Their movements are normally slow and methodical, but their long legs can carry them away remarkably quickly when they are alarmed. The animals don't like a dry atmosphere and usually spend the daytime in shady spots.

Harvestmen are not fussy eaters, although they prefer meat to vegetables, and, unlike spiders, they don't care if it is already dead. Small insects, spiders, earthworms, millipedes and other harvestmen all figure largely in their diet. Small snails are enthusiastically seized by several species and they are the main foods of *Trogulus* and some other soil-dwelling harvestmen. Young woodlice are regularly eaten, despite their repellent fluids, and the harvestmen also chew fungi, fallen fruit and dung. Food is usually detected by touching it with the sensitive second pair of legs – there is no smelling from a distance – and the animals ensure that these legs remain in good shape by washing them regularly. All legs and palps are washed by drawing them carefully through the chelicerae, and this is one of the few things that harvestmen do with any grace: balancing on tip-toe while systematically drawing each leg through the jaws is quite a performance. Although a harvestman can enjoy life quite well with six, five or even just four legs, it can't survive for long without at least one of the second pair.

Prey is simply trampled on and held down by the legs while the chelicerae tear it up. The bases of the palps and front legs help to crush the food, and

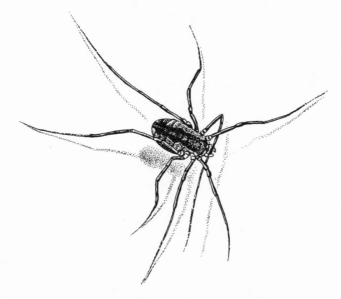

A harvestmen carefully cleans a leg by drawing it through the chelicerae.

then it is all shovelled into the mouth; unlike the spiders, the harvestmen are not limited to liquefied food. They also like a drink and cannot survive for more than a few days without water. They regularly lap up rain and dew.

Casual sex

Female harvestmen are often a bit larger than their mates, as in the spiders, but the sexes are otherwise very similar. Apart from a bit of palp-holding, designed to get the animals into the right position, there is little courtship or foreplay and the male gets on with the job as quickly as possible. Unlike the spiders and other arachnids, he goes in for copulation in the traditional way, using a penis – and a pretty long one at that. Snaking from its pouch on the underside of his body, it gropes the female and, with a bit of help from her palps or chelicerae, soon finds the way in. Sperm delivery is immediate and the whole process is often over in a few seconds.

Harvestmen are promiscuous creatures and both partners may begin new affairs as soon as they separate, although it is quite common for them to mate repeatedly with the same partner. One exhibitionist in America managed it 29 times, with a variety of partners, in abut 150 minutes. Parthenogenesis or virgin birth occurs in some species – notably the European *Megabunus diadema*, in which the males are heavily outnumbered by the females.

Annual life cycles

Harvestman eggs are usually spherical and up to a millimetre across and the female uses her long ovipositor to lay them in small batches in soil or debris. The hatchlings undergo seven or eight moults as they grow up. In the temperate regions most harvestmen complete their lives within a year. The eggs are usually laid in the autumn and they hatch in the spring to produce a new generation of adults in late summer. Some spring-maturing species, including *Megabunus diadema*, pass the winter as slumbering sub-adults. Soil-living harvestmen such as *Trogulus* and *Nemastoma* take more than a year to mature. With conditions remaining fairly constant in the soil, these animals have no distinct breeding season and adults can be found at all times of the year.

The harvestmen have many enemies, including ground beetles, centipedes, toads and shrews. Other harvestmen are important enemies. Birds eat them, but not in large numbers. The repellent glands (see page 118) deter many potential predators – including ants and spiders, which usually cut harvestmen from their webs very quickly. Many harvestmen carry bright red parasitic mites, which attach themselves to the inter-segmental

membranes of the legs and suck out the body fluids, although they do not seem to do a lot of harm.

Harvestmen in the garden

About a dozen species can be found quite regularly in British gardens. *Leiobunum rotundum* with its very long, hair-like legs and tiny body is common on walls and, together with *Opilio parietinus*, is often found in outside toilets, to which it is attracted by the moisture. *O. parietinus*, recognized by its strongly speckled underside, is common on walls and fences and is just about the only harvestman found in the middle of London. *Odiellus spinosus*, which has a rather squat and flattened body and a distinctly truncated rear to its saddle, likes to lurk under pinks and other low-growing plants – which it protects from slugs, caterpillars and other pests. It also frequents the bases of walls, where it is often joined by *Phalangium opilio*. The latter, whose male has horn-like projections on its chelicerae, has a brilliant white underside. The rather variable *Mitopus morio*, common in wilder gardens as well as in hedgerows and woodlands, is one of the most widely distributed of all harvestmen. It even occurs on the Arctic tundra. Lacking the ballooning abilities of spiders, most harvestmen are poor travellers and the majority of species have rather restricted distributions, although several species that have become associated with human settlements have travelled the globe with man and settled in many regions. *P. opilio* and *O. parietinus*, for example, both thought to have originated around the Black Sea and the eastern Mediterranean, are now widely distributed in Eurasia and North America. *Dicranopalpus ramosus*, recognized by its forked palps, is rarely found away from gardens in Britain and may well have arrived with garden plants from its native south-west Europe.

Further reading

W. S. Bristowe, *The Comity of Spiders* (2 Vols, Ray Society, London, 1939, 1941)

W. S. Bristowe, *The World of Spiders* (Collins, London, 1958)

M. Chinery, *The Natural History of the Garden* (Collins, London, 1977)

M. Chinery, *Garden Creepy Crawlies* (Whittet, London, 1986)

J. A. Coddington & H. W. Levi, *Systematics and Evolution of Spiders [Araneae]* (Annu. Rev. Ecol. Syst., 1991, 22, 565–92)

R. F. Foelix, *Biology of Spiders* (Harvard, Cambridge, Mass., 1982)

P. D. Hillyard & J. H. P. Sankey, *Harvestmen* (Linnean Society of London, E. J. Brill, 1989)

D. Jones, *The Country Life Guide to Spiders of Britain and Northern Europe* (Hamlyn, London, 1983)

B. Y. Main, *Spiders* (Collins Australian Naturalist Library, Sydney, 1976)

W. Nentwig (ed.), *Ecophysiology of Spiders* (Springer-Verlag, Berlin, 1987)

R. & K. Preston-Mafham, *Spiders of the World* (Blandford, London, 1984)

M. J. Roberts, *The Spiders of Great Britain and Ireland* (3 Vols, Harley Books, Colchester, 1985, 1987)

T. H. Savory, *The Spider's Web* (Warne, London, 1952)

T. H. Savory, *Arachnida* (Academic Press, London, 1977)

P. N. Witt & J. S. Rovner (eds.), *Spider Communication: Mechanisms and Ecological Significance* (Princeton University Press, Princeton, N. J., 1982)

The British Arachnological Society caters for anyone interested in spiders and other arachnids. The Society publishes a regular journal – the *Bulletin of the British Arachnological Society* – which contains a wide variety of articles on arachnids from all over the world. The address is:
c/o 71 Havant Road, Walthamstow, London E17 3JE.

Index

Page numbers in bold indicate illustrations

If you have enjoyed this book, you might be interested to know about other Whittet natural history titles:

BADGERS
by Michael Clark
with illustrations by the author

BATS
by Phil Richardson
with illustrations by Guy Troughton

DEER
by Norma Chapman
with illustrations by Diana Brown

EAGLES
by John A. Love
with illustrations by the author

FALCONS
by Andrew Village
with illustrations by Darren Rees

FROGS AND TOADS
by Trevor Beebee
with illustrations by Guy Troughton

GARDEN CREEPY-CRAWLIES
by Michael Chinery
with illustrations by Guy Troughton

HEDGEHOGS
by Pat Morris
with illustrations by Guy Troughton

MICE AND VOLES
by John Flowerdew
with illustrations by Steven Kirk

OTTERS
by Paul Chanin
with illustrations by Guy Troughton

OWLS
By Chris Mead
with illustrations by Guy Troughton

POND LIFE
by Trevor Beebee
with illustrations by Phil Egerton

PUFFINS
by Kenny Taylor
with illustrations by John Cox

RABBITS AND HARES
by Anne McBride
with illustrations by Guy Troughton

ROBINS
by Chris Mead
with illustrations by Kevin Baker

SEALS
by Sheila Anderson
with illustrations by Guy Troughton

SNAKES AND LIZARDS
by Tom Langton
with illustrations by Denys Ovenden

SQUIRRELS
by Jessica Holm
with illustrations by Guy Troughton

STOATS AND WEASELS
by Paddy Sleeman
with illustrations by Guy Troughton

URBAN FOXES
by Stephen Harris
with illustrations by Guy Troughton

WHALES
by Peter Evans
with illustrations by Euan Dunn

WILDCATS
by Mike Tomkies
with illustrations by Denys Ovenden

Each title is priced at £7.99 at time of going to press. If you wish to order a copy or copies, please send a cheque, adding £1 for post and packing, to Whittet Books Ltd, 18 Anley Road, London W14 0BY. For a free catalogue, send s.a.e. to this address.